# Candy Recipes
# & Other Confections

# Candy Recipes
# & Other Confections

BY
MAY B. VAN ARSDALE
AND
RUTH PARRISH CASA EMELLOS

*with an Introduction by*
NATALIE K. FITCH

DOVER PUBLICATIONS, INC.

NEW YORK

Published in Canada by General Publishing Company, Ltd., 30 Lesmill Road, Don Mills, Toronto, Ontario.

Published in the United Kingdom by Constable and Company, Ltd., 10 Orange Street, London WC 2.

This Dover edition, first published in 1975, is an unabridged. and unaltered republication of the work first published in 1941 by M. Barrows & Company, Inc. under the title *Our Candy Recipes & Other Confections*.

International Standard Book Number: 0-486-23129-1
Library of Congress Catalog Card Number: 74-83765

Manufactured in the United States of America
Dover Publications, Inc.
180 Varick Street
New York, N. Y. 10014

With Appreciation

We Dedicate this Book to:

DAN MONROE

Assistant Chief, Bureau of Home Economic

Washington, D. C.

and to:

MARY I. BARKER

Director of Home Economics, the Kellogg Company

Battle Creek, Michigan

Two of Our Former Colleagues

Who Have Helped to Make

This Book Possible

*ACKNOWLEDGMENT*

*Thanks are due to the Cookery Staff of
the Department of Household Arts and Sciences of
TEACHERS COLLEGE, COLUMBIA UNIVERSITY
for Permission to Use Many Recipes Found to
Be Especially Successful in Classroom Work*

# Preface

APPARENTLY nearly everybody likes candy because, according to the report of the United States Chamber of Commerce, we ate two billion pounds in the year 1939. This is an appalling amount—enough to fill fifty thousand box cars.

There is hardly a home where candy is not made—at least occasionally—and there are few cookery courses which do not include one or two candy lessons. But the kinds of candy commonly made are few in number. There is little realization of the possibilities of home-made candy, of the wide range of varieties, delicious and attractive enough to compete with those purchased in the Fifth Avenue shops. Yet such candies can be made in the home or in the classroom without special training or skill and with the simple equipment ordinarily found there.

Many of the recipes in this book were originally published under the title *Our Candy Recipes* and to those have been added several new chapters not only of candies but of other sweets as well. All of these recipes have been tested many times in the laboratory as well as in the classroom. Much effort has been spent in making the recipes simple and accurate. The object has been to eliminate the trial and error method and to make them sufficiently detailed to insure success without the waste of materials.

We have omitted the more elaborate types of commercial candies because we realize that they cannot be successfully duplicated without special training and equipment.

We wish you the enjoyment in using this book which we have had in making it.

MAY B. VAN ARSDALE
RUTH PARRISH CASA EMELLOS

# Contents

# Introduction

## By Natalie K. Fitch

NOTE: *This introduction is designed primarily for teachers and for mature candy makers who are interested in the scientific answer to the question, "Why does sugar behave this way."*

*A more popular treatment of the same question for less mature readers will be found in Chapter I, "The Magic of the Candy Pan."*

THERE are few processes in the realm of cookery as fascinating as that of candy making, in which, from so simple a product as a plain sugar syrup or a syrup containing a few added ingredients, so large a variety of candies is prepared. The fundamental difference among these varieties is in the crystalline structure of the candy which ranges all the way from that which is coarsely crystalline as in rock candy through the fine crystal structure characteristic of fudge and fondant to that entirely devoid of sugar crystals, as in caramels and brittles.

With the exception of rock candy, all of the crystalline varieties of candy should possess a creamy consistency which is imparted to them by the presence of very many and very small sugar crystals. A knowledge of how these tiny sugar crystals are obtained is important for success in candy making.

When a syrup of granulated sugar and water is heated, it begins to boil at approximately the temperature of boiling water; but on further heating and evaporation of water the syrup becomes progressively more concentrated with the result that the temperature continues to increase. It follows therefore that the particular temperature reached indicates the sugar concentration in the syrup and is an important factor in determining the particular type of candy obtainable. This will be discussed later.

Upon removal of the boiling sugar syrup from the heat, it begins to cool and, if left undisturbed and cooled to a sufficiently low temperature, will become highly supersaturated. If the crystallization of sucrose (granulated sugar) is brought about from such a highly supersaturated sugar solution the resulting candy will be of a creamy consistency. This is due to the fact that when the supersaturated solution is beaten, many minute sucrose crystals begin to form and with continued beating and cooling more and more sucrose comes out of the solution, and either forms new crystals or deposits upon those already formed, causing them to grow to a relatively large size.

This tendency of crystals to grow can be minimized by continuing the beating of the syrup, thus keeping the crystals apart until crystallization is complete at the temperature at which the candy is to be held. The resulting candy is a mass of tiny sucrose crystals surrounded by a relatively small amount of syrup from which the crystals were formed. The syrup is now a saturated sugar solution and the relative amount of it to the crystalline mass depends upon the temperature employed in heating the sugar syrup and is responsible, in part, for the degree of hardness of the candy.

In the preparation of rock candy, in which large sucrose crystals are desired, the concentrated sugar syrup is stirred when it has cooled sufficiently to become just supersaturated and then the stirring is discontinued. By this procedure, the crystals which first form from the cooling syrup are relatively few in number and as the syrup cools they are given an opportunity to grow as others come out of solution and deposit upon them.

Another way to obtain FINE crystals in candy is to have present in the supersaturated solution from which crystallization is to be brought about some material which prevents the growth of sucrose crystals. These materials, often called interfering agents, inhibit the crystallization of sucrose and, because of their viscous nature, tend to coat the surface of sucrose crystals and thus prevent their growth into large ones. Corn syrup, which is a mixture of water, dextrin, maltose, and dextrose, is often added to the sugar syrup before it is heated in order to function as an interfering agent.

Another such agent is invert sugar, a small amount of which is produced from the sucrose during heating by the process of hydrolysis. Invert sugar is a syrup composed of equal amounts of levulose and dextrose and, in addition to interfering with the growth of sucrose crystals, it is hydroscopic in nature, a property which aids in keeping the candy moist. The extent of the hydrolysis of sucrose is increased by the presence of an acid or an acid salt, which explains the use of a small amount of vinegar, lemon juice, or cream of tartar in candy recipes. Fat, egg proteins, and milk solids all possess the property of coating sucrose crystals and thus contribute to the creaminess of the candy structure. It follows that too large an amount of interfering material will so greatly interfere with sucrose crystallization that the disproportionate amount of sugar syrup to crystalline sugar will give a product too soft to be handled.

This property is made use of in making such candies as caramels and nougats, the non-crystalline soft structure of which is produced by the presence of a sufficient amount of interfering material to completely prevent sucrose crystallization. Recipes for these candies have larger amounts of corn syrup than those for crystalline candies and in addition include relatively large amounts of butter, milk or milk solids. The temperature to which the candy is cooked is higher than for the crystalline candies in order to produce a product sufficiently concentrated to have the desired degree of firmness.

The non-crystalline hard structures of candies such as butterscotch, taffies, and brittles is obtained by heating the sugar syrup to such a high temperature that practically all of the water is evaporated and the resulting candy is composed almost entirely of melted sucrose. This product does not crystallize on cooling until a long period has elapsed, possibly several weeks. The possibility of eventual crystallization is minimized by introducing either corn syrup or invert sugar to act as an interfering agent.

Since the most desirable concentration of sugar syrup is different for the various kinds of candies it is essential to have some means of measuring it. A method commonly used is the cold water test, in which a small amount of the boiling syrup is dropped into cold water, allowed to remain for about a minute, and the firmness of the ball which forms noted upon removal.

As the concentration of the syrup increases the firmness of the ball increases and, with experience, a relationship may be observed between the firmness of the ball and the desired concentration. However, this cold water test is not reliable, since it places too great a dependence upon the individual's judgment as to the character of the ball.

The use of a thermometer in conjunction with the cold water test affords the ONLY accurate method for determining the concentration of the sugar syrup. The accompanying table gives the temperature and the character of the ball formed in cold water for all types of candies. Since the specific temperature at which a ball of a given consistency is formed varies according to the composition of the syrup a range of temperatures is given in each case.

If a syrup contains added corn syrup a ball of a given consistency is formed at a lower temperature, while one containing invert sugar forms such a ball at a higher temperature than if it were obtained from a syrup composed of sucrose and water alone. These facts explain the different temperatures given in different recipes for the same kind of candy. For example, a fudge recipe including corn syrup will give a soft ball at a lower temperature than will one containing cream of tartar to produce some invert sugar as the product boils.

Brown sugar contains a small amount of invert sugar, therefore a recipe calling for this sugar does not include either corn syrup or an acid ingredient and requires boiling to a higher temperature within a given range to give a ball of the proper consistency in the cold water test.

# TEMPERATURES AND TESTS FOR SYRUP AND CANDIES *

| PRODUCT | TEMPERATURE OF SYRUP AT SEA LEVEL (INDICATING CONCENTRATION DESIRED) | | STAGE OF CONCEN- TRATION DESIRED | BEHAVIOR AT STAGE DESIRED |
|---|---|---|---|---|
| | *degrees F.* | *degrees C.* | | |
| Syrup ............ | 230 to 234 | 110 to 112 | Thread | The syrup spins a two-inch thread when dropped from fork or spoon. |
| Fondant ⎫ Fudge ⎬ ............ Penuchi ⎭ | 234 to 240 | 112 to 115 | Soft ball | The syrup when dropped into very cold water forms a soft ball which flattens on removal. |
| Caramels ...... | 244 to 248 | 118 to 120 | Firm ball | The syrup when dropped into very cold water forms a firm ball which does not flatten on removal. |
| Divinity ⎫ Marshmallows ⎬ Nougat ⎬ ...... Popcorn balls ⎬ Salt-water taffy ⎭ | 250 to 265 | 121 to 130 | Hard ball | The syrup when dropped into very cold water forms a ball which is hard enough to hold its shape, yet plastic. |
| Butterscotch ⎫ ......... Taffies ⎭ | 270 to 290 | 132 to 143 | Soft crack | The syrup when dropped into very cold water separates into threads which are hard but not brittle. |
| Brittle ⎫ ...... Glacé ⎭ | 300 to 310 | 149 to 154 | Hard crack | The syrup when dropped into very cold water separates into threads which are hard and brittle. |
| Barley sugar ......... Caramel ......... | 320 338 | 160 170 | Clear liquid Brown liquid | The sugar liquefies. The liquid becomes brown. |

*Chart taken from "Terminology Used in Food Preparation," American Home Economics Association, Washington, D. C., 1936, p. 19.

A simplified table for more popular use will be found on page 6.

# Candy Recipes & Other Confections

# Chapter 1:

## THE MAGIC OF THE CANDY PAN

The introduction deals with the science of sugar cookery and explains what appears to be the magic of the candy pan with which this chapter deals. What child would believe that the little sugar house at which he has gazed, with his nose glued to the window of the confectionery store, was once plain sugar such as he used on his morning cereal? This would seem to him no less a miracle than the changing of the pumpkin into Cinderella's coach. And he would be right! Even the scientist who is familiar with the many wonderful changes that take place when sugar is cooked, still marvels at the ever increasing varieties of candies resulting from the magic of the candy pan.

It seems a long way from the nut brittle made by the simple caramelization of sugar to the sugar château with its many turrets, its semitransparent window panes, and its brown roof, all made from sugar cooked to different temperatures.

But the difference between these, as between many candies, depends upon just this—the cooking of sugar and water to different temperatures and the handling of it in different ways. By changing the temperature and the methods of manipulation we get varieties of fondant, taffies, brittles, and clear hard candies.

Let's put some sugar and water in the saucepan over the flame and see what magic we can work. First, the sugar dissolves. When it begins to boil our thermometer registers about the temperature of boiling water (212° F.).

As the boiling continues, the temperature keeps going up and the syrup gets noticeably thicker. Although analysis would show that with each degree of the thermometer a

**3**

change has taken place, the first important stage in the making of candy is the so-called "soft ball stage," about 236° F.–240° F. If we take some of the syrup from our pan at this stage we can make from it soft, creamy fondant for bonbon centers, mints, or creams. The candy continues to cook and the mercury goes up. The syrup passes through the "firm ball stage" (246° F.–250° F.) to the "hard ball stage" (265° F.), and from syrup taken out now we make taffy. At the "crack stage," still higher (290° F.), we make butterscotch, and then higher yet (300° F.–310° F.), brittles and hard candies.

From the sugar with which we started we have made from our one saucepan, cream peppermints, centers for chocolate creams, white taffy, brittles, and lollypops.

By adding other ingredients to our sugar and cooking to different temperatures, we can make a great variety of candies with no more effort and skill than we needed for our fondant.

The important points in candy making are carefully measured ingredients, the temperature to which the sugar is cooked and the manipulation of the cooked candy. Sometimes the whole fate of the candy—whether it is grainy or smooth—depends on the temperature at which it is beaten.

**Creamy Candies.**—In certain types of candy, such as fudge, penuchi, or fondant, we want the sugar crystals to be as tiny as possible, so minute that they can scarcely be felt in the mouth. This makes the candy smooth and "creamy." Such texture is achieved by observing two rules:

I. Cook the candy to a very definite temperature. The only way to measure temperature accurately is by using the thermometer. An approximate temperature can be secured by the cold water test, but this may not be right within three or four degrees. A small variation in temperature will not make so much difference in a taffy or a brittle as in a fondant or a fudge, where every degree counts. This is why we have so much poor fondant and fudge while taffy is usually good.

II. Cool the candy before beginning to beat it. When the candy is beaten while hot, large sugar crystals are formed and the candy is "grainy." A great deal of fudge is of this kind.

An added safeguard against grainy candy is the use of a small proportion of corn syrup. This helps to prevent the formation of large crystals of sugar. The same effect can be obtained by cream of tartar, lemon juice, vinegar, or acetic acid. Any one of these ingredients will produce a candy of smooth texture, but for general use the corn syrup is more dependable. Since all of these give similar results they can be used interchangeably; the amount required varies in each case and must be definitely worked out.

**Taffies and Hard Candies.**—In taffies, brittles, and clear candies we do not want any crystallization of the sugar, because this would make the clear candies cloudy and the brittles sugary. To avoid this crystallization we put in a larger proportion of corn syrup, we stir the candies only enough to keep them from burning during the cooking, we turn them out quickly when they are done, and we do not scrape the saucepan too closely. When sugar crystals are formed on the sides of the saucepan we wash them off with cheesecloth dipped in cold water, because if one sugar crystal is poured out with the candy it may cause crystallization of the whole batch.

**The Cold Water Test.**—For many years the cold water test has been used to determine when a candy is done. This test should be made with water that is really cold. Take out about a teaspoonful of the cooking candy and drop into the cold water. When the hot syrup is cooled by the water it thickens and can be formed into balls of varying degrees of hardness expressed in terms used in the table below.

Of course this test is not so accurate as the thermometer, but it is a gauge which can be used by the experienced with more or less success.

The simplified table below shows the temperatures to

which different types of candies should be cooked and the cold water test for each.

| TYPE OF CANDY | TEMPERATURE | COLD WATER TEST |
|---|---|---|
| Fudge, penuchi, operas, maple creams, etc. | 234 or 238° F. | soft ball |
| Fondant | 238 or 240° F. | soft ball |
| Caramels | 246 or 248° F. | firm ball |
| Taffies | 265 – 270° F. | hard ball |
| Butterscotch, toffee, etc. | 290 – 300° F. | crack |
| Brittles | 300 – 310° F. | hard crack |
| Clear hard candies | 310° F. | hard crack |

**The Thermometer.**—A thermometer is essential in order to obtain uniformly good results in candy making. Experience can teach you to know when candy is "done," either by its appearance, or by the "feel" of the "cold water test." But in gaining this experience, you may waste much material and time. Even when you have once gained the experience, unless you make candy frequently you lose your skill.

The temperature to which any candy should be cooked is very important and the thermometer is a device for determining this accurately.

Either of two types of thermometer may be purchased—the chemical thermometer or the thermometer specially designed for candy making, with a metal back and an adjustable hook which fits over the side of the candy pan. The advantages of this latter type are that it need not be held in place while the candy is cooking, and it is not likely to break because of the protection of the metal back. Its disadvantages are that it is difficult to clean, and it cannot be used with small quantities of candy in the saucepan because the bulb will not be covered. This type of thermometer should be moved from time to time along the side of the pan when the candy is being stirred, so that it will not scorch where the thermometer hangs.

The chemical thermometer has the advantage of being easily cleaned, easily read, and practical for use with small amounts of candy. It can also be used for other purposes. Its only disadvantages are that it is more easily broken and it must be held in the candy, as it cannot be hung on the side of the kettle.

The chemical thermometer should be laid on a damp cloth

when taken from the hot candy syrup to keep it from rolling and to prevent breakage. If laid on a cold slab or table it may break. It should be cleaned and put into a case when not in use.

The Fahrenheit thermometer has been used in our candy making. The centigrade thermometer may be used, if desired, but all of the temperatures given must be changed to the centigrade scale.

The formulas for changing from one scale to the other follow:

Centigrade temperature multiplied by nine fifths plus 32 equals Fahrenheit.

Fahrenheit temperature minus 32 and multiplied by five ninths equals Centigrade.

**Standardizing the Thermometer.**—When a new thermometer is bought it should be tested immediately for accuracy by inserting the bulb in sufficient rapidly boiling water to cover it. The thermometer will register 212 degrees Fahrenheit if all conditions such as atmospheric pressure, etc., are standard on that day. Slight variations therefore must be allowed, but if the thermometer registers far above or below 212 degrees it should be exchanged for a more accurate one.

The only way to determine whether the boiling point has been reached is to be sure that a stationery point has been reached no matter how long the thermometer remains in the boiling water.

**Saucepans.**—Choose a saucepan of the proper size for the kind of candy to be made. Remember that all candy "boils up" and space must be allowed for this.

The saucepan should have a smooth surface, because any rough spot may cause the candy to stick and burn. Copper, aluminum or agate should be used.

**Spoons and Spatulas.**—Wooden spoons are desirable for candy making, because they do not become too hot to handle when left in the cooking candy. It is also easier to beat with a wooden spoon, because the handle does not cut into the hand.

For measuring use standard cups and spoons. All measurements are level.

A medium sized spatula is very useful. The flexible blade is an aid in scraping the candy from pans and platters, in raising brittle from the slab, and in taking such candy as caramels and fudge from the pans.

**Fondant Paddles.**—A clean putty knife, with a blade of medium width, can be used as a fondant paddle. Special fondant paddles of wood, or of metal with wooden handles, can be purchased. Even a tablespoon may be used if fondant paddles cannot be procured.

**Measuring Cups.**—It is better to use a standard measuring cup than a tea cup. Many tea cups contain less than a half pint, and, if used, will throw other measurements out of proportion.

**Slabs, Baking Sheets, Platters, or Pans.**—A marble slab is desirable for candy making, but not essential. It furnishes a smooth, level surface. It is especially desirable when dropping fondant patties, making lollypops, or pouring brittles. You may have an old-fashioned, marble-topped table or bureau, from which the slab can be removed for use in candy making. The tray from under the burners of the gas stove, if level, makes a good substitute for a marble slab.

Tin baking sheets, such as are used for cookies, are desirable when slabs are not available, because they have a larger surface than the ordinary cake pan. They should be inverted for brittles and similar candies when the edge of the pan would be in the way.

A platter is smooth and therefore useful when a slab or large baking sheet is not available for the types of candies mentioned above. When a flat surface is necessary, the platter should be inverted. A platter, uninverted, can be used for taffy which is to be taken out and pulled, or for fondant which is to be beaten, but should not be used for such things as fudge or caramels.   The latter types of candy take the shape of the utensil into which they are poured, and therefore should be poured into a pan with square corners.

**Professional Equipment.**—Even for home use, a slab with metal candy bars is useful.   By means of the bars you can regulate the size of your block and hence its thickness.   When the candy is firm the bars can be removed, and it is ready for cutting without the struggle of getting it out of the pan. If you decide to go into candy making on a commercial scale you will need additional equipment.   The best thing to do is to visit a wholesale confectioners' supply house and select what will meet your individual needs.

# Chapter 3:

## WHAT WE PUT INTO CANDY

**Sugar.**—Granulated sugar is to be used in all recipes unless otherwise specified.

When brown sugar is employed, try to obtain the light brown, which is neither strong in flavor nor sticky. Brown sugar contains some acid which may cause milk to curdle, and therefore, when they are used together, the mixture must be stirred constantly during cooking. Light brown sugar gives a better flavor than dark brown but if it is not obtainable satisfactory results can be had by using one part of granulated sugar to three or four parts of dark brown.

If confectioners' sugar is used, be sure it is free from lumps.

**Molasses.**—Do not use the dark, strong molasses, unless you are partial to its peculiar flavor. The majority of persons prefer the more delicate flavor of medium or light molasses.

**Corn Syrup.**—There are two kinds of corn syrup in general use—the light and the dark. Do not use the dark when the light is called for, because its stronger flavor and dark color may not be desirable.

Corn syrup is used in many recipes to prevent the forming of large sugar crystals instead of the cream of tartar or lemon juice commonly called for. When measuring corn syrup be sure the measurements are accurate. A spoonful means a level spoonful, not all that may cling to the bottom of the spoon. If too much is used the resulting candy will be soft.

**Butter.**—If butter is not too expensive, it is desirable in candy because of its flavor. The pans should always be greased with butter, because some of the grease from the pan will stick to the candy and this will be tasted first when the candy is eaten. When butter costs too much, use a substitute.

**11**

When greasing pans use only enough fat to give a light coating to the pans. Use equal measures in substituting.

APPROXIMATE WEIGHTS AND MEASURES

TO BE USED AS A GUIDE IN PURCHASING MATERIALS

| MATERIAL | WEIGHT OF ONE CUPFUL | NUMBER OF CUPS TO A POUND |
|---|---|---|
| Almonds | 4 ounces | 4 |
| Butter | 8 ounces | 2 |
| Butterine | 8 ounces | 2 |
| Cherries, candied | 8 ounces | 2 |
| Cocoa | 4½ ounces | 3½ |
| Cocoanut, desiccated | 3⅓ ounces | 5 |
| Corn syrup | 12 ounces | 1⅓ |
| Dates | 5¾ ounces | 2⅘ |
| English walnuts, shelled | 3¾ ounces | 4¼ |
| Peanuts, shelled | 6¼ ounces | 2½ |
| Pecans, shelled | 3¾ ounces | 4¼ |
| Pistachio nuts | 4 ounces | 4 |
| Raisins | 5 ounces | 3⅓ |
| Sugar, brown | 6 ounces | 2⅔ |
| Sugar, confectioners' | 5⅓ ounces | 3 |
| Sugar, granulated | 8 ounces | 2 |

**Milk.**—Unless otherwise stated, fresh milk is meant when "milk" is called for in a recipe. If fresh milk cannot be secured, use unsweetened evaporated milk, diluted according to directions given on the can, or powdered milk, mixed with water.

When cream is called for we mean whipping cream. When this is not available, use a thinner cream, or top milk, and add two tablespoons of butter to each cup. When a recipe calls for cream, the substitution of milk will not give the same results.

**Cocoa and Chocolate.**—In recipes where chocolate is called for, cocoa may usually be substituted, in the proportions of three tablespoons of cocoa and three-quarters of a tablespoon of butter, for each square (ounce) of chocolate. The extra butter is added because the chocolate contains more fat than the cocoa.

# Chapter 4:

## QUICK AND EASY CANDIES

The modern trend in cookery is toward foods that are quickly and easily prepared and yet are really good to eat. This tendency is reflected in candy making when those who have a sweet tooth want something in a hurry even if it is not always so good in texture as the product which takes longer to make. It should be remembered that in the long run, the cooked sugar candies are more acceptable to the majority of people.

Children often like to begin their candy making experience with the uncooked products which do not require the patience and skill of sugar cookery. This is why these easy recipes come early in the book.

Many people today are using ready-mixed fudge preparations which produce fudge simply by the addition of water. You may be satisfied with your favorite brand of the mix, but by using the following recipes you can have a variety of flavors with little more effort and very little more time spent in the preparation than when you use the prepared mix.

The basis of all uncooked creamy candies is confectioners' sugar. Any other variety will give too coarse a grain. Best results are obtained by using a rich recipe; that is, one which contains a rather large amount of butter, eggs, chocolate, cream or condensed or evaporated milk.

In using the recipes for creamy candies use the amount of liquid and flavoring materials called for and add a little less than the amount of sugar called for. After kneading the mixture well it should be the consistency of soft fudge. If more sugar is required add it gradually, for too much sugar will make the candy coarse grained and dry.

If the candy is to be cut into squares press it firmly into the pan and pat the top with the palm of the hand until it looks

**13**

smooth and glossy.  It is not necessary to place these candies in the refrigerator but they should stand an hour or so before cutting.

Any of the creamy candies may be moulded into balls and used as centers for bonbons or for stuffing fruits.  Small balls may be rolled in finely chopped nuts, colored candies, cocoa, etc., as described under cooked fondant on page 21.

The keeping quality of uncooked candies seems to be as good as that of similar varieties which are cooked.

Uncooked fondant cannot be successfully softened and dropped into thin patties.  It is necessary to have the cooked fondant for these.

Since no temperatures are involved in these uncooked candies, a variation in the amount of ingredients will not be disastrous to the result.  In the cooked candies all measurements should be made with great accuracy.

## QUICK FUDGE

| LARGE RECIPE | SMALL RECIPE |
|---|---|
| Chocolate, 4 ounces | Chocolate, 2 ounces |
| Butter, ¼ cup | Butter, 2 tablespoons |
| Egg, 1 | Egg, 1 yolk |
| Condensed milk, ¼ cup | Condensed milk, 2 table- |
| Confectioners' sugar, 1 pound | spoons |
| Vanilla, 1 teaspoon | Confectioners' sugar, ½ pound |
| Nuts, ½ cup | Vanilla, ½ teaspoon |
| | Nuts, ¼ cup |

Melt the chocolate and butter over hot water.  Add the egg, condensed milk and vanilla and mix.  Add the other ingredients, mix well and then knead together.  Press into a lightly buttered pan. Chill and cut into squares.

Yield (large recipe): weight 2 pounds.

## QUICK FUDGE II

Chocolate, 4 ounces
Butter, 2 tablespoons
Evaporated milk or cream, ¼ cup
Vanilla, 1 teaspoon
Eggs, 1
Salt, ⅛ teaspoon
Confectioners' sugar, 1 pound
Nuts, ½ cup

Melt the chocolate and butter over hot water. Add the milk, vanilla, egg, slightly beaten, and salt and mix well. Add the confectioners' sugar, mix well and knead until smooth. Press into a lightly buttered pan. Cool, remove and cut into squares.

Yield: weight 2 pounds.

## QUICK FUDGE III

Mashed potato, ¼ cup
Salt, ⅛ teaspoon
Chocolate, 3 ounces

Butter, 1 tablespoon
Vanilla, ½ teaspoon
Confectioners' sugar, 1 pound

Melt the chocolate and butter over hot water. Add thoroughly mashed potato, salt and vanilla and mix. Add confectioners' sugar, mix and then knead. Press into a lightly buttered pan, cool, remove from pan and cut into squares.

Yield: weight 1¼ pounds.

## COCOANUT SURPRISES

Marshmallows, ¼ pound (about 15)
Water, 1 tablespoon
Cocoanut, chopped, ¾ cup
Walnuts, ½ cup (about 20 halves)

Add the water to the marshmallows and melt them in the top of a double boiler. Using a fork, dip each nut into the melted marshmallows and cover it completely. Roll in the chopped cocoanut. Leave the balls in the air a few minutes to dry.

Pitted dates, any candied fruit or other nuts may be used for the centers.

Chopped pecans or walnuts may be used in place of the cocoanut for covering each one.

Yield: weight 6 ounces; 20 pieces.

## CARAMEL WALNUT SQUARES

> **Butter, 2 tablespoons**
> **Dark caramel syrup, 3 tablespoons**
> **Condensed milk, 2 tablespoons**
> **Vanilla, 1 teaspoon**
> **Salt, ⅛ teaspoon**
> **Confectioners' sugar, 1 pound**
> **Chopped walnuts, ¾ cup**

Melt the butter, add the caramel syrup,* condensed milk and vanilla. Mix and add the salt and sugar. Knead in the chopped nuts. Press into a lightly buttered pan, cool, remove from pan and cut into squares.

Yield: weight about 1¼ pounds.

## PEANUT BUTTER FUDGE OR FONDANT

> **Mashed potato, ⅔ cup**
> **Peanut butter, ½ cup**
> **Salt, ⅛ teaspoon**
> **Confectioners' sugar, 1 pound**

Mash the potato thoroughly and knead in all of the other ingredients. Press into a lightly buttered pan and allow it to stand for an hour before cutting.

Yield: weight about 1¾ pounds.

This candy may be used as fondant centers and may be

---

* Directions for making the caramel syrup will be found on page 157.

coated with dipping chocolate or with one of the chocolate fudges. It may also be made into a layer candy by combining it with a fudge. To do this put a thin layer of chocolate fudge into a pan; cover it with a thin layer of peanut butter fudge, press the two together well and put a thin layer of chocolate fudge on top. Press into the pan well and allow it to stand an hour before cutting.

### UNCOOKED FONDANT

**Egg whites, 1**
**Evaporated milk or cream, 2 tablespoons**
**Confectioners' sugar, 1 pound**
**Flavoring and coloring matter**

Beat the egg white slightly, add the milk or cream and the confectioners' sugar. Flavor and color as desired. The candy may be divided and each part flavored and colored differently. Knead the flavored candy well and shape into small balls. Garnish with nuts or roll the balls in chopped nuts. Balls flavored with almond extract and rolled in chopped toasted almonds are very good.

Yield: weight 1 pound 2 ounces.

### QUICK MOCHA FUDGE

| LARGE RECIPE | SMALL RECIPE |
|---|---|
| Strong coffee, ½ cup | Strong coffee, ¼ cup |
| Vanilla, ½ teaspoon | Vanilla, ¼ teaspoon |
| Butter, 2 tablespoons | Butter, 1 tablespoon |
| Cocoa, 2 tablespoons | Cocoa, 1 tablespoon |
| Confectioners' sugar, 6 cups | Confectioners' sugar, 3 cups |
| Chopped nuts, ⅔ cup | Chopped nuts, ⅓ cup |

Add the butter to the hot coffee. Add the vanilla and then the other ingredients. Mix and knead well. Press into a lightly buttered pan. Chill and cut into squares.

Yield (large recipe): weight 17 ounces.

## CEREAL BALLS OR SQUARES

| LARGE RECIPE | SMALL RECIPE |
|---|---|
| Sweet chocolate, 4 ounces | Sweet chocolate, 2 ounces |
| Butter, 4 tablespoons | Butter, 2 tablespoons |
| Marshmallows, ½ pound (about 30) | Marshmallows, ¼ pound (about 15) |
| Vanilla, ½ teaspoon | Vanilla, ¼ teaspoon |
| Dry, ready to eat cereal, 6 cups | Dry, ready to eat cereal, 3 cups |

Melt the chocolate, butter and marshmallows in the top of a double boiler. Add vanilla, mix well and pour over the cereal, blend well to coat the individual grains of cereal. Shape into balls or press into lightly greased pans and when cool turn out and cut into squares.

The chocolate may be omitted, if desired.

One-half cup chopped pecans, walnuts, peanuts or cocoanut may be added.

Popped corn may be substituted for the cereal.

Yield (large recipe): weight 1 pound.


## CHOCOLATE CREAMS I

Sweet Dipping Chocolate, ½ pound
Evaporated milk, ⅔ cup
Vanilla, ½ teaspoon or cinnamon, ¼ teaspoon

Melt the chocolate in a double boiler, add the evaporated milk and the flavoring, mix well and cook about 15 minutes. Stir occasionally during the cooking time. Drop from the tip of a teaspoon on waxed paper or on a smooth buttered surface or cool and shape into balls with the hands. Garnish the drops with chopped nuts or half a walnut or pecan. Roll the balls in chopped nuts, chopped cocoanut, chocolate sprinkles, cocoa or colored decorettes. Chill before serving.

Yield: weight 10 ounces; about 20 drops or balls.

## CHOCOLATE CREAMS II

**Sweet dipping chocolate, 4 ounces**
**Butter, 1 teaspoon**
**Condensed milk, ½ cup**
**Vanilla, ½ teaspoon or cinnamon, ⅛ teaspoon**

Melt the chocolate and butter in a double boiler. Add the condensed milk and cook until thick. Add the flavoring. Drop from the tip of a teaspoon on waxed paper or on a buttered smooth surface to make chocolate drops or cool and shape into balls. Garnish the drops or balls as directed in chocolate creams I.

Yield: weight 9 ounces; 24 patties or balls.

## CHOCOLATE COCOANUT DROPS

**Sweet or semi-sweet dipping chocolate, 4 ounces**
**Shredded cocoanut, ¼ pound**

Melt the chocolate over warm, not hot, water. Chop the cocoanut and add it to the melted chocolate. Mix well and drop from the tip of a teaspoon on waxed paper or on a smooth buttered surface. Chill and remove.

Yield: weight 8 ounces; 24 small drops.

**General Directions.**—The primary object in fondant making is to produce a creamy mass in which the crystals are of the smallest possible size.

Fondant of a fine, smooth texture can be made from sugar and water, but success is more certain if corn syrup is added, or if some acid is added to change some of the sugar into a form which retards crystallization.

The acids in most common use in fondant making are:

| | |
|---|---|
| cream of tartar | acetic acid |
| lemon juice | vinegar |

Their effect upon the texture of fondant is practically the same. Cream of tartar is the acid in most general use because of its lack of distinctive flavor and the fact that it is easy to handle and is usually on hand in the kitchen. The taste of vinegar may be detected and lemon juice or acetic acid usually have to be specially purchased.

For a fondant recipe containing 2 sups of sugar use:

| | |
|---|---|
| **Either corn syrup** | **2 tablespoons** |
| or cream of tartar | ⅛ teaspoon |
| or vinegar | ½ teaspoon |
| or lemon juice | ½ teaspoon |
| or acetic acid (36%) | 3 drops |

Corn syrup is more likely to give consistently good results than the acids. With the acids there is the danger that a prolonged time of cooking will produce a fondant which is very soft and sticky.

Care must be taken to *cook* the fondant to the right temperature and to *cool* it to the right temperature before beginning beating.

Detailed directions for the cooking of fondant are given under the recipe for white fondant.

Suggestions for the use of fondant will be found in Chapter VI, "What Can be Done With Fondant."

## WHITE FONDANT

| LARGE RECIPE | SMALL RECIPE |
|---|---|
| Sugar, 2 cups | Sugar, 1 cup |
| Water, 1¼ cups | Water, ¾ cup |
| Light corn syrup, 2 table-spoons | Light corn syrup, 1 table-spoon |
| Vanilla, 1 teaspoon or a few drops of a flavoring oil | Vanilla, ½ teaspoon or a few drops of a flavoring oil |

Put the sugar, water, and corn syrup into a saucepan and cook, stirring constantly until the sugar is dissolved. Remove the spoon and do not stir the candy again during the cooking.

When the candy begins to boil, cover the saucepan and cook for three minutes. The steam formed washes down any sugar crystals which may be thrown on the sides of the saucepan. Remove the cover and continue cooking.

From time to time wash away any sugar crystals which appear on the sides of the saucepan. For this purpose a fork, covered with cheesecloth and dipped in cold water may be used.

Cook until the temperature 238° F. is reached.

If a firmer fondant is desired for molding, cook to 240° F. The fondant cooked to 238° F. is suitable for cake frosting, mints, cocoanut drops, fudge de luxe, etc.

Remove from fire and pour at once on a cold, wet platter. Cool to 110° F. (lukewarm). Beat with a fondant paddle or a spatula until the fondant becomes white and creamy. Knead until the mass is smooth and no lumps remain.

Put away in a crock or glass jar and allow to "ripen" for

two or three days before using. The fondant can be kept for three or four weeks if it is kept tightly covered.

Cold water test when fondant is cooked to 238° F.: soft ball.

Yield (large recipe): weight—one pound.

## CHOCOLATE FONDANT

Use recipe for white fondant (above) adding either 1½ oz. chocolate or 3 tablespoons cocoa to the sugar mixture before cooking and boil to 238° F. Proceed as for white fondant.

## COFFEE FONDANT

| LARGE RECIPE | SMALL RECIPE |
|---|---|
| Sugar, 2 cups | Sugar, 1 cup |
| Strong coffee, strained, 1¼ cups | Strong coffee, strained, ¾ cup |
| Light corn syrup, 2 table-spoons | Light corn syrup, 1 table-spoon |
| Vanilla, 1 teaspoon | Vanilla, ½ teaspoon |

Make strong coffee and strain it through cheesecloth so that it will be absolutely free from grounds.

Put the sugar, coffee, and corn syrup into a saucepan and cook, following general directions for fondant making under white fondant.

## MAPLE FONDANT

| LARGE RECIPE | SMALL RECIPE |
|---|---|
| Sugar, 2 cups | Sugar, 1 cup |
| Maple syrup, ⅔ cup | Maple syrup, ⅓ cup |
| Water, ¾ cup | Water, ½ cup |
| Vanilla, 1 teaspoon | Vanilla, ½ teaspoon |

Put the sugar, syrup, and water into a saucepan and cook, following the directions given under white fondant. This fondant is softer than white fondant, hence it should be cooked to 240° F.

## CARAMEL FONDANT

| LARGE RECIPE | SMALL RECIPE |
| --- | --- |
| Sugar, 2 cups | Sugar, 1 cup |
| Caramel syrup, ⅔ cup | Caramel syrup, ⅓ cup |
| Water, ¾ cup | Water, ½ cup |
| Vanilla, 1 teaspoon | Vanilla, ½ teaspoon |

If you do not have caramel syrup on hand it can be made by following the directions given on page 157.

Put the sugar, caramel syrup, and water into a saucepan and cook, following the directions given under white fondant. Cook until the temperature 240° F. is reached. The caramel tends to make the fondant softer and more sticky.

## LEMON FONDANT

| LARGE RECIPE | SMALL RECIPE |
| --- | --- |
| Sugar, 2 cups | Sugar, 1 cup |
| Water, 1 cup | Water, ¾ cup |
| Light corn syrup, 2 table-spoons | Light corn syrup, 1 tablespoon |
| Grated rind of ½ lemon | Grated rind of ¼ lemon |
| Lemon juice, 3 tablespoons | Lemon juice, 1½ tablespoons |

Wash the lemon and grate the rind, using only the yellow part, as the white gives the candy a bitter taste.

Put the sugar, water, and corn syrup into a saucepan and cook, stirring until the sugar is dissolved. Continue cooking, without stirring, until the temperature 248° F. is reached. If any sugar crystals form on the side of the pan during the cooking, wash them away with a wet cloth.

Remove the syrup from the fire. Mix together the lemon juice and rind, and spread them over a damp platter. Pour the hot syrup at once over the fruit mixture. Do not stir. Cool to 120° F. (lukewarm). Beat until creamy. This is somewhat difficult to beat at first because the fruit juice does not blend easily with the candy. A long beating is required. When the fondant becomes thick and can be handled, knead until smooth.

Put away in a covered jar until wanted.

Cold water test when fondant reaches 248° F.: firm ball.

Yield (large recipe): weight—one pound.


## ORANGE FONDANT

| LARGE RECIPE | SMALL RECIPE |
|---|---|
| Sugar, 2 cups | Sugar, 1 cup |
| Water, 1 cup | Water, ¾ cup |
| Light corn syrup, 2 table-spoons | Light corn syrup, 1 table-spoon |
| Orange juice, 3 tablespoons | Orange juice, 1½ tablespoons |
| Grated rind of 1 orange | Grated rind of ½ orange |
| Lemon juice, 1 tablespoon | Lemon juice, ½ tablespoon |

Put the sugar, water, and corn syrup into a saucepan and cook, following general directions for the cooking of white fondant, except for the temperature to which the syrup is cooked.

Cook until the temperature 252° F. is reached. Remove from fire. Mix together the orange juice, rind, and lemon juice. Spread over a cold platter. Pour the hot syrup over the fruit mixture. Do not stir.

Cool to 120° F. (lukewarm) and beat, following general directions for the beating, kneading, and storing of fondant.

It is somewhat difficult to beat this fondant because the thick syrup does not blend easily with the fruit juices.

Cold water test when the fondant reaches 252° F.: very firm ball.

Yield (large recipe): weight—one pound.

## BROWN SUGAR FONDANT

| LARGE RECIPE | SMALL RECIPE |
|---|---|
| Granulated sugar, 1 cup | Granulated sugar, ½ cup |
| Brown sugar, 1 cup | Brown sugar, ½ cup |
| Water, 1¼ cups | Water, ¾ cup |
| Vanilla, 1 teaspoon | Vanilla, ½ teaspoon |

Put the white sugar, brown sugar, and water into a saucepan and cook, following the directions for making given under white fondant.

No corn syrup is needed for this fondant, the acid in the brown sugar making the fondant creamy.

## BUTTER FONDANT

| LARGE RECIPE | SMALL RECIPE |
|---|---|
| Sugar, 2 cups | Sugar, 1 cup |
| Milk, ¾ cup | Milk, ½ cup |
| Light corn syrup, 1 tablespoon | Light corn syrup, ½ tablespoon |
| Butter, 1 tablespoon | Butter, ½ tablespoon |
| Vanilla, 1 teaspoon | Vanilla, ½ teaspoon |

Put all of the ingredients except the butter and the vanilla into a saucepan and cook, stirring until the sugar is dissolved.

Continue cooking until the temperature 238° F. is reached. Occasional stirring will be required to prevent butter fondant from scorching.

Remove from fire, add butter, and allow to stand until butter is melted. Stir only enough to mix the butter through the mass and pour on a platter which has been rinsed with cold water.

When cool (110° F.) add vanilla and begin beating with a fondant paddle. Follow general directions for the beating and kneading of fondant.

This is not quite so smooth as the white fondant. It has

a slightly caramel flavor and a rich, cream color.  It makes delicious centers for pecan rolls or for chocolates.

Cold water test when fondant reaches 238° F.: soft ball.

Yield (large recipe): weight—one pound.

## ORIENTAL CREAMS

| LARGE RECIPE | SMALL RECIPE |
|---|---|
| Sugar, 2 cups | Sugar, 1 cup |
| Egg white, 1 | Egg white, ½ |
| Water, 1 cup | Water, ¾ cup |
| Glycerine, ¼ teaspoon | Glycerine, ⅛ teaspoon |
| Light corn syrup, 1 table-spoon | Light corn syrup, ½ table-spoon |
| Vanilla, 1 teaspoon | Vanilla, ½ teaspoon |

Put the sugar, water, and corn syrup into a saucepan and cook, stirring constantly until the sugar is dissolved.  Remove the spoon and do not stir the candy again during the cooking.

When the candy begins to boil, add glycerine, cover the saucepan, and cook for three minutes.  The steam formed washes down any sugar crystals which may be thrown on the sides of the saucepan.  Remove the cover and continue cooking.

From time to time wash away any sugar crystals which appear on the sides of the saucepan.  For this purpose a fork covered with cheesecloth and dipped into cold water may be used.  Cook until the temperature 240° F. is reached.

Remove from fire and pour at once on a cold, wet platter. Cool to 110° F. (lukewarm).

Spread the stiffly beaten egg white over the cooled fondant.  Beat with a fondant paddle or spatula until the fondant becomes white and creamy.  Add vanilla and work until the mass is smooth and no lumps remain.

The fondant should be shaped at once for centers for chocolates and put in a cold place.  Because the fondant softens upon standing it should be dipped as soon as possible after shaping.

This kind of fondant is especially adapted for cream centers for chocolates because it becomes very soft upon ripening. Directions for chocolate dipping are given in Chapter XVIII.

Cold water test when syrup reaches 240° F.: soft ball.

Yield (large recipe): one and three-quarters cups fondant; weight—fifteen ounces.

# Chapter 6:

## WHAT CAN BE DONE WITH FONDANT

There has been some prejudice against fondant as a home-made candy because too often it has been merely flavored with vanilla, and then made into little balls sandwiched between nuts. This combination is very sweet, and dries out quickly.

Such candies are uninteresting, but the makers should be blamed rather than the fondant. Fondant can be used as the foundation for many candies which are interesting and delicious.

**Fondant Patties.**—The simplest way of giving character to fondant is by adding flavor and color and by making it into patties—the round cream peppermints and wintergreens which are used so often as after-dinner candies. These can be made in two ways, dropped or molded.

For either kind of patties the fondant must be melted over hot water. It is better to melt a small amount of fondant (about one cup) at a time. With large amounts there is danger of making the last of the patties sugary because of crystallization. This is caused by the hardening of the fondant on the sides of the pan, or by the stirring necessitated by the dipping.

Keep the water under the fondant (in the bottom part of the double boiler if you are using one) just below the boiling point. Stir the melting fondant enough to blend it. If the fondant is very soft it should be dried over the hot water for about ten minutes so that the patties will hold their shape. It can be tested by dropping a small amount on waxed paper to see that it becomes firm.

If the fondant is rather stiff before melting, it should not be allowed to stand over the hot water after it is well softened.

28

It may be necessary to add a teaspoon of hot water so that it can be dropped easily. The fondant should be soft, for dryness causes patties to be covered with white spots.

When the fondant is melted and ready for use, the coloring and flavoring should be added with as little stirring as possible. Your own judgment will have to be used for the amounts of coloring and flavoring, but they should both be delicate. Flavoring oils are better to use than essences because they are stronger, and a few drops will give the desired flavor. In adding an essence it is sometimes necessary to add so much that the consistency of the fondant is affected.

Peppermints are usually left white, unless some color is desired for a special color scheme. Pink is the accepted color for wintergreen patties, green for spearmint or lime, bright red for cinnamon or clove, and pale yellow for lemon. For coffee, orange, or maple patties, use fondants made according to directions for these special flavors.

**Dropped Patties.**—The dropped patties are made by dropping the melted, flavored fondant from the tip of a teaspoon onto waxed paper or a greased, flat surface. For after-dinner candies these are usually no larger in size than a quarter. As soon as firm, they should be loosened and lifted because if they stand too long they will break when taken up. To make dropped patties even in size and perfectly round it is necessary to have a level, smooth surface and to pour the melted fondant from the tip of the spoon. If the fondant is thoroughly melted the patties will be smooth on top. If it is beginning to cool and harden slight peaks will form as the patties are dropped. To prevent this, re-melt the fondant over hot water and continue dropping it.

**Molded Patties.**—A very satisfactory way to shape patties is by dropping them into the smallest sized muffin tins or patty pans, making a one-quarter of an inch layer. The pans should be lightly buttered or dusted with cornstarch, so that the patties will slip out easily. If the fondant is thin enough, pour the melted fondant directly from the top of the double boiler into the pans, instead of dropping it out by spoonfuls. This enables you to work more quickly and there is less stirring of the fondant than when the patties are dipped out. When the patties are cold and firm, invert the pans on a clean, folded tea towel; tap the bottoms lightly, and the patties will fall out in perfect shapes. The soft towel will prevent them from breaking.

These patties are thicker than when dropped from the spoon, and therefore remain creamy longer.

The patties can be made attractive by simple decorations which are discussed in Chapter XIX.

**Fondant Kisses.**—For these kisses, melt the fondant according to directions given for fondant patties. To the melted fondant, add flavoring, coloring, if desired, and either nuts or cocoanut. Add a third of a cup of broken nut meats or desiccated cocoanut to a cup of fondant. This mixture will be stiffer than that used for the cream patties, and when dropped from the spoon should form a little mound on the waxed paper or the greased platter. If the kisses are too soft to hold their shape when dropped, cool the mixture before dropping, or cook it a little longer over the hot water.

Either maple, coffee, or brown sugar fondant can be used for the kisses and these are usually more popular than those made from the plain vanilla fondant.

**Kisses in Chocolate.**—These are made by dipping the lower part of the kisses in melted coating chocolate. Follow general directions for melting chocolate, given in Chapter XVIII. Put the melted chocolate to be used for dipping into a sauce dish, having it only about three-eighths to one-half of an inch deep—the depth you wish the chocolate on the sides of the kisses. Set the kisses, one by one, into the chocolate, lift out carefully, and place on the oil cloth covered boards used for chocolate coating, or on waxed paper.

The kisses may be taken from the chocolate dipping dish

and set into chopped nuts. Blanched pistachio nuts are especially pretty on account of their color.

**Fondant Loaves.**—For fondant loaves the fondant is not melted, but fruits and nuts are kneaded into it. Knead only enough to mix the fruit through the mass. If too much mixing is done the fondant will be discolored. The beauty of a fondant loaf is in having the fruit colors stand out in the light candy.

Do not chop the fruit into very small pieces. When the loaf is cut, a slice of a cherry will be more attractive than small bits of red which have lost their identity.

The following are good combinations for fondant loaves:

(1) Candied cherries, pineapple, and pistachio nuts. This is especially pretty in Christmas candies because of the red and green colors.

(2) Dates, figs, and nuts.

(3) Raisins, cherries, and almonds.

(4) Desiccated cocoanut and candied apricots.

A loaf can be shaped with the hands or molded in a pan. It is easier to make a loaf of regular shape when a pan is used. Allow the fondant mixed with fruits to stand until firm. Turn out. Slice.

Especially interesting is the two layer loaf, made as a layer cake. Cut two pieces of fondant loaf mixture the same size, about one and one-quarter inches thick, six inches long, and two inches wide. Cover one piece with melted coating chocolate, lay the other piece on top, and coat the whole with chocolate. When cold, slice. Nuts may be sprinkled over the chocolate coating while it is still soft.

**Neapolitan Fondant.**—A fondant loaf may be made in three layers of different colors. These may be put together with chocolate if desired. Nuts and fruits may be put in one or more layers.

A good combination is a layer of maple fondant, a layer of pale pink fondant, with candied cherries, and a layer of butter fondant with pistachio nuts.

## SYRUP FOR SATIN FONDANT COATING

> **Sugar, ½ cup**
> **Water, ½ cup**
> **Light corn syrup, 2 tablespoons**
> **Glycerine, 1 tablespoon**

Put the sugar, corn syrup, and water into a saucepan and cook, stirring, until the sugar is dissolved. Continue cooking, without stirring, until the temperature 220° F. is reached. Skim, and, if necessary, strain through cheesecloth.

Cool to 180° F. and add glycerine. Put into a sterilized glass jar or bottle; seal and keep in a cool place for future use. This need not stand, but can be used immediately after being made.

This syrup gives the fondant coating a gloss and helps to keep it soft and mellow.

## SATIN FONDANT COATING

| LARGE RECIPE | SMALL RECIPE |
|---|---|
| **Vanilla fondant, 1 cup** | **Vanilla fondant, ½ cup** |
| **Coating syrup, 1½ teaspoons** | **Coating syrup, ¾ teaspoon** |

Heat the fondant over water which is just below the boiling point. Stir so that the fondant will melt evenly and that which is in the bottom will not become liquid. Add the coating syrup and stir only enough to blend. When all the fondant is melted and thin enough to make a smooth coating, dip into it the nuts or bonbon centers.

If cream centers are to be coated, shape them in small balls, and then press them until the top is slightly peaked. Drop into the fondant with the peak side down. Press into the coating until completely covered. Remove with a fork or a wire candy dipper. In taking the fork from the dipping pan scrape it on the edge of the pan to remove superfluous fondant. The bonbon will lie on the fork with the top or peaked side up. Drop it from the fork to the board. As the fork leaves the candy a small amount of coating will cling to it, and this by a turn of the fork can be made into the little fancy twist which gives the bonbon a professional air.

The cream centers should be made quite small. Don't forget that when covered with fondant they will be much larger.

If the fondant becomes too thin over the hot water, remove it from the water until it thickens.

It is more satisfactory to work with a small amount of fondant. Not more than one cup should be melted at a time, and, if you have a small utensil so that the fondant will be deep enough to cover the bonbons, one-half of a cup is better.

Dip only one bonbon at a time. If a fondant center remains in the warm coating, it will lose its shape.

The fondant coating is especially desirable when given soft pastel tints. When the coating fondant is ready for use, add a drop or two of coloring and stir enough to mix so there are no streaks. Do not make the colors too vivid, as this is the failing of the amateur.

**Fondant Covered Raisins.**—Use satin fondant coating, recipe for which is given on page 32.

Melt the satin fondant coating according to directions given in the recipe.

Clean the raisins and remove stems and bits of seed. If raisins are allowed to remain in the fondant they will discolor it, hence they should be dropped in one at a time. Press the raisin into the coating until completely covered and remove with a fork or a wire candy dipper.

Lay the coated raisin on heavy waxed paper or chocolate dipping boards, or drop it into finely chopped nuts and roll until completely covered.

These are more attractive for boxes when dipped into tinted fondant. Especially pretty are raisins dipped in pink satin coating fondant and rolled lightly in chopped pistachio nuts or browned almonds, so that you can catch glimpses of the color.

**Fondant Animals.**—Every child likes animal crackers, but they are more popular than ever when coated with fondant.

Maybe no one ever saw a purple cow, but a pale pink lamb or a white elephant will please a child.

Use satin fondant coating, for which recipe is given on page 32. Dip the animals, one by one, according to directions given under satin fondant coating. To make the upper surface of the aniamls smooth, lift them from the coating with the top uppermost and slip the fork from underneath.

The animal can be made more realistic by decorations of melted chocolate, drawn on with a toothpick.

**Fondant Coated Nuts.**—Use satin fondant coating, recipe for which is given on page 32.

Select large perfect nut meats. If almonds are to be used, blanch them (see directions on page 117) and heat them in the oven until crisp and delicately browned. Freshen pecans or walnuts by crisping them in a moderate oven.

Melt the satin fondant coating, according to directions given in the recipe. Drop several nuts into the fondant, press them into the coating until completely covered, and remove one at a time with a fork or wire candy dipper.

When taken from the coating, the nuts may be laid immediately on the chocolate dipping boards or heavy waxed paper, or they may be dropped into chopped nuts and rolled until completely covered.

The coated nuts may be sprinkled with tiny candies, or rolled in chopped, desiccated cocoanut.

## MAPLE COATING

| LARGE RECIPE | SMALL RECIPE |
|---|---|
| Maple sugar, 1 cup | Maple sugar, ½ cup |
| Granulated sugar, 1 cup | Granulated sugar, ½ cup |
| Water, 1¼ cups | Water, ¾ cup |
| Light corn syrup, 1 tablespoon | Light corn syrup, ½ tablespoon |
| Glycerine, 1½ teaspoons | Glycerine, ¾ teaspoon |

Break the maple sugar into pieces and put it into a saucepan with the granulated sugar, water, and corn syrup. Cook slowly, stirring until the sugar is dissolved. Then add the glycerine and continue cooking, without stirring, until the temperature 238° F. is reached. Should sugar crystals form on the sides of the pan wash them away with a piece of wet cloth.

Remove from the fire and pour on a cold, wet platter. Cool to 110° F. (lukewarm). Beat with a fondant paddle or spatula until the fondant becomes light and creamy. Knead until the mass is smooth and no lumps remain.

This can be used at once for coating or put away and kept for several days.

For coating, melt over hot water, following the directions given under satin fondant coating, page 32. Add the coating syrup, in the proportions given, one and one-half teaspoons of the syrup to each cup of fondant.

Cold water test when maple coating reaches 238° F.: soft ball.

# Chapter 7:

## FUDGE, PENUCHI, AND OPERAS

**General Directions for Fudge.**—Fudge is one of the most popular of the candies made at home. There is a tradition that it originated in one of the colleges for women. Whether or not this is true, fudge has become an undeniable part of college life. Perhaps this is because the recipe can be varied in so many ways and the cooking can be done more or less carelessly and yet something passably edible will result.

However, there is no need for making fudge only "passably edible" when by following certain rules the fudge will be good every time. The original fudge always contained chocolate. Although now "maple" or "brown sugar" fudge is sold, containing no chocolate, there are many who think that this is not real fudge.

The best fudge should be of a very smooth texture, not in the least granular, and soft enough to cut into even pieces without breaking. The pieces should be from one-half to three-fourths of an inch thick. If the fudge is too thin it dries out quickly.

The use of corn syrup is advised because the fudge will have a smoother texture and will keep moist for a longer time than when sugar is used alone.

Probably the most important factor in making good fudge is the temperature at which it is beaten. When removed from the fire it should be allowed to cool to 110° F. (lukewarm) before it is stirred at all. Do not even stir in the butter. If stirred while hot, large sugar crystals will form and the fudge will be grainy. If allowed to cool before being stirred, the sugar crystals that form will be so small that the fudge will be as smooth as any one could desire.

Sometimes fudge curdles. This is due to the action of the

36

acid of the chocolate on the milk. This curdling can be prevented by constant stirring during the first part of the cooking until the mass is well blended. Should curdling occur, the only remedy is constant stirring during the cooking process. This prevents the formation of larger curds and breaks up those already formed.

The recipes given here call for one square of chocolate to a cup of sugar. This makes a fudge of medium darkness. For a more "chocolaty" fudge use additional chocolate.

If corn syrup is used a long beating is necessary. Many people make the mistake of turning out their fudge before it has been sufficiently beaten. Fudge should be beaten until a small amount dropped from the spoon holds its shape. It can then be put into the pans. It may not be so smooth on top as the fudge turned out sooner but it will have a creamier texture, which is more important.

## COLLEGE FUDGE

LARGE RECIPE

Sugar, 2 cups
Milk, ⅔ cup
Chocolate, 2 squares
   (2 ounces)
Light corn syrup, 2 table-
   spoons
Butter, 2 tablespoons
Vanilla, 1 teaspoon

SMALL RECIPE

Sugar, 1 cup
Milk, ½ cup
Chocolate, 1 square (1 ounce)
Light corn syrup, 1 table-
   spoon
Butter, 1 tablespoon
Vanilla, ½ teaspoon

Break the chocolate into small pieces, so that it will melt easily.

Put the sugar, milk, chocolate, and corn syrup into a saucepan and cook slowly, stirring until the sugar is dissolved. Continue cooking, stirring often to prevent burning, until the temperature 236° F. is reached.

Remove from the fire, add butter, and set aside to cool without stirring. When the candy has cooled to 110° F.

(lukewarm), add vanilla and begin to beat. Continue beating until the fudge loses its shiny look and a small amount dropped from the spoon will hold its shape. Pour into slightly greased pans.

Be sure to beat the fudge until it has lost its sticky consistency before pouring it into the pans. Fudge made with corn syrup requires longer beating than other fudge.

It may be necessary to knead the fudge in order to put it into the pans.

When cold cut into squares.

Cold water test when fudge reaches 236° F.: soft ball.

Yield (large recipe): number of pieces—thirty-six (one inch square, at least one-half of an inch thick); weight—one and one-quarter pounds.

## BROWN SUGAR FUDGE I

LARGE RECIPE

Brown sugar, 1 cup
Granulated sugar, 1 cup
Milk, ⅔ cup
Chocolate, 2 squares
  (2 ounces)
Butter, 2 tablespoons
Vanilla, 1 teaspoon

SMALL RECIPE

Brown sugar, ½ cup
Granulated sugar, ½ cup
Milk, ½ cup
Chocolate, 1 square (1 ounce)
Butter, 1 tablespoon
Vanilla, ½ teaspoon

Break the chocolate into small pieces so that it will melt easily. Put the sugar, milk, and chocolate into a saucepan and cook slowly, stirring constantly, until the temperature 236° F. is reached.

Remove from fire, add butter without stirring, and set aside to cool. When the candy has cooled to 110° F. (lukewarm), add vanilla and begin beating. Continue beating until the fudge has lost its shiny look and a small amount dropped from the spoon will hold its shape.

Pour into greased pans.

When cold cut into squares.

Cold water test when candy reaches 236° F.: soft ball.

Yield (large recipe): number of pieces—thirty-six (one inch square and at least one-half of an inch thick); weight—one and one-quarter pounds.


## VARIATIONS IN THE COLLEGE FUDGE RECIPE

**Brown Sugar Fudge II.**—Brown sugar may be substituted for white in the college fudge recipe. The directions for making are the same, except that the fudge must be stirred constantly during the cooking or the acid of the brown sugar will curdle the milk. Cook to 238° F. instead of 236° F. because the acid of the brown sugar produces invert sugar and makes a softer candy.

**Peanut Butter Fudge.**—One-fourth cup of peanut butter may be substituted for the two tablespoons of butter called for in college fudge. The same directions for cooking are followed, the peanut butter being added after the candy is cooked, before setting it aside to cool. Do not try to stir in the peanut butter until the candy has reached 110° F. (lukewarm).

**Nut Fudge.**—One-half cup of broken nut meats may be added to the college fudge or the brown sugar fudge. These should not be put in until the fudge is almost ready to pour into the pans because they make the beating harder. Black walnuts, English walnuts, or pecans are especially good.

**Cocoanut Fudge.**—Fresh or desiccated cocoanut may be added to the fudge instead of nuts. If fresh cocoanut is used be sure that it is thoroughly dried before combining it with the candy or it will make the fudge too soft. To the college fudge recipe, add half a cup of cocoanut just before putting the beaten fudge into the pans.

**Marshmallow Fudge.**—A cup of marshmallows may be cut into small pieces with the scissors and stirred into the fudge just before turning it into the pans. When making marshmallow fudge, use three squares of chocolate instead of two in the college fudge recipe because the darker fudge furnishes a contrast both in flavor and color with the bland, white marshmallows.

## SUPER FUDGE

| LARGE RECIPE | SMALL RECIPE |
|---|---|
| Sugar, 2 cups | Sugar, 1 cup |
| Milk, ⅔ cup | Milk, ½ cup |
| Chocolate, 4 squares (4 ounces) | Chocolate, 2 squares (2 ounces) |
| Light corn syrup, 2 table-spoons | Light corn syrup, 1 table-spoon |
| Fondant, ¾ cup | Fondant, ⅓ cup |
| Butter, 2 tablespoons | Butter, 1 tablespoon |
| Vanilla, 2 teaspoons | Vanilla, 1 teaspoon |

Break the chocolate into small pieces so that it will melt easily. Put the sugar, milk, chocolate, and corn syrup into a saucepan and cook slowly, stirring until the sugar is dissolved. Continue cooking, stirring to prevent burning, until the temperature 236° F. is reached.

Remove from fire, add butter, and set aside to cool. When lukewarm (110° F.) add vanilla and fondant, and beat until the fudge has lost its glossy appearance and can be molded. The fondant should be of the consistency desired in the finished fudge. If the fondant is too soft the fudge cannot be molded. In case the fondant is very soft it can be dried in the upper part of the double boiler or the fudge can be cooked to 237° F.

Suggestions for the use of super fudge are given on pages 41-42.

Cold water test when fudge reaches 236° F.: soft ball which does not quite hold its shape.

Yield (large recipe): weight—one and two-thirds pounds.

## SUGGESTIONS FOR THE USE OF SUPER FUDGE

**Fudge Marbles.**—Mold the fudge into balls not more than three-fourths of an inch in diameter. If larger the marbles art not nearly so attractive. These marbles can be treated in different ways. They may be rolled in desiccated cocoanut or in chopped nuts. Blanched almonds or pistachio nuts are especially pretty. Marbles rolled in cocoa are popular because they give a finishing touch to a candy box, their dull reddish color contrasting pleasantly with the glossy chocolates. The very small round colored candies which are often called "hundreds and thousands" are very effective for a coating.

The marbles may have centers of hazel nuts or of other kinds of candy, such as butter fondant.

**Fudge Roly-Poly.**—On a smooth, greased surface pat out a piece of fudge not larger than four by six inches and about one-third of an inch thick. On top of this place a piece of fondant of the same thickness and shape, but a little smaller in size. Roll as in making a jelly roll, folding the white fondant inside. The finished roll should show no fondant and be perfectly smooth. Allow to stand until firm. Cut, slanting the knife, into slices about one-half inch thick. Wipe the knife after each slice is cut, so that the fondant will not be discolored by the fudge.

**Fudge Logs.**—Make a roll of coffee or butter fondant, about five and one-half inches in length and three-fourths of an inch in diameter. Lay this on a sheet of fudge, pressed out as for a roly-poly. Wrap the fudge round the fondant center. Roll lightly, using both hands, until smooth and regular in shape. Then roll in chopped nuts, pressing hard enough to imbed the nuts in the fudge.

Slice, slanting the knife, making the pieces about three-fourths of an inch thick. Wipe the knife after each slice is cut so that the fondant center will not be discolored.

**Fudge Double Decker.**—Fudge double decker is a two layer combination, one layer being super fudge and the second layer some contrasting candy, as butter fondant, divinity, coffee fondant, or tutti frutti fondant.

Into a slightly buttered pan, press the fondant or light colored candy, making a layer about three-fourths of an inch thick. On top of this put a layer of super fudge. Allow to stand until firm. Turn out of the pan, coat the top of the light layer with melted dipping chocolate. Before the chocolate hardens sprinkle with chopped nuts or small candies.

Cut into squares or diamond shapes.

**Fudge Bacon Rolls.**—Prepare a fudge double decker, using vanilla fondant and super fudge. When firm turn out of the pan. Cut into very thin slices and roll.

Three layers may be used instead of two.

## PENUCHI

**General Directions for Penuchi.**—Penuchi is a creamy candy belonging to the fudge family. Therefore it follows the general rules for temperatures of cooking and cooling which are laid down in the directions for making fudge.

With the brown sugar there is more of a tendency for the milk to curdle so that constant stirring is necessary throughout the cooking.

| LARGE RECIPE | SMALL RECIPE |
|---|---|
| Brown sugar, 3 cups | Brown sugar, 2 cups |
| Milk, 1 cup | Milk, 2/3 cup |
| Butter, 2 tablespoons | Butter, 1 tablespoon |
| Vanilla, 1½ teaspoons | Vanilla, 1 teaspoon |
| Nut meats, 1½ cups | Nut meats, 1 cup |

Put the sugar and milk into a saucepan and cook, stirring constantly, until the temperature 236° F. is reached.

Remove from fire, add butter, and set aside, without stirring, to cool. When lukewarm (110° F.) beat until thick and creamy. Add vanilla and nut meats, and mix thoroughly. Pour into slightly greased pans.

When cold cut into squares.

The flavor of pecans or walnuts is especially good with the penuchi although other nuts may be used.

Cold water test when candy reaches 236° F.: soft ball.

Yield (large recipe): number of pieces—eighteen; weight —one and one-third pounds.

## VARIETIES OF PENUCHI

**Coffee Penuchi.**—For coffee penuchi use one cup of strong boiled coffee, carefully strained so as to be free from grounds, instead of the milk called for in the large penuchi recipe. Follow the same general directions for cooking. The blend of brown sugar and coffee flavors is delicious.

**Ginger Penuchi.**—Use the large recipe for penuchi and follow the general directions for making, only leave out the nuts and in their place use one-fourth of a cup of finely cut, preserved ginger.

## SUPER PENUCHI

| LARGE RECIPE | SMALL RECIPE |
|---|---|
| Brown sugar, 3 cups | Brown sugar, 2 cups |
| Thin cream, 1 cup | Thin cream, ⅔ cup |
| Butter, 1 tablespoon | Butter, ½ tablespoon |
| Vanilla, 1½ teaspoons | Vanilla, 1 teaspoon |
| Black walnuts, ⅔ cup | Black walnuts, ½ cup |

Put the sugar and cream into a saucepan and cook, stirring constantly until the temperature 236° F. is reached. Remove from the fire, add butter, and set aside to cool without stirring.

When lukewarm (110° F.) beat until thick and creamy. Add vanilla and nut meats and mix thoroughly. Pour into slightly greased pans. When cold cut into squares.

This candy is delicious in combination with the super fudge in double deckers. It also can be made into marbles or used as centers for chocolates.

If the cream is very rich use part milk or omit the butter. Cold water test when the candy reaches 236° F.: soft ball. Yield (large recipe): number of pieces—eighteen; weight —one and one-fourth pounds.

## "OPERAS"

**General Directions for Operas.**—Opera creams are very rich candies and expensive to make. They have excellent keeping qualities owing to the large amount of fat in the cream, hence they can be made several weeks before they are to be used. This makes them valuable for packing in boxes which are to be sent to a distance.

They are usually cut in pieces the size of caramels and may be wrapped as caramels.

Operas also belong to the fudge family, therefore they follow the general rules for temperatures of cooking and cooling which are laid down in the directions for making fudge.

## "LIGHT OPERAS"

| LARGE RECIPE | SMALL RECIPE |
|---|---|
| Sugar, 2 cups | Sugar, 1 cup |
| Heavy cream, ¾ cup | Heavy cream, ⅓ cup |
| Milk, 1 cup | Milk, ½ cup |
| Light corn syrup, 1 table-spoon | Light corn syrup, ½ table-spoon |
| Salt, ⅛ teaspoon | Salt, $\frac{1}{16}$ teaspoon |
| Vanilla, 1 teaspoon | Vanilla, ½ teaspoon |
| Pecan meats, 1 cup | Pecan meats, ½ cup |

Put all of the ingredients except the nuts and vanilla into a saucepan and cook, stirring constantly, until the temperature 236° F. is reached.

Remove from the fire and set aside to cool. When lukewarm (110° F.) add vanilla and beat until the candy becomes creamy and loses its shiny appearance. A long beating is needed. Add nuts and pour into slightly greased pans.

When cold, cut into pieces a little less than an inch square. Cold water test when candy reaches 236° F.: soft ball.

Yield (large recipe): number of pieces—thirty-six; weight —one and one-eighth pounds.

## "GRAND OPERAS"

| LARGE RECIPE | SMALL RECIPE |
|---|---|
| Sugar, 2 cups | Sugar, 1 cup |
| Light corn syrup, 3 table-spoons | Light corn syrup, 1½ table-spoons |
| Cream, ½ cup | Cream, ¼ cup |
| Milk, 1½ cups | Milk, 1 cup |
| Salt, ¼ teaspoon | Salt, ⅛ teaspoon |
| Vanilla, 1 teaspoon | Vanilla, ½ teaspoon |

Put all of the ingredients except the vanilla into a saucepan and cook until the temperature 238° F. is reached. It is better to cook this mixture rather slowly so that some of the sugar may caramelize. During the cooking stir constantly to prevent burning. Candies containing cream scorch easily.

When done turn out on a cold platter. Cool until lukewarm (110° F.). Beat with a fondant paddle until it becomes thick and creamy and has lost its shiny appearance. A long beating is needed.

Press into pans. When cold cut into squares.

This candy is smooth and creamy in texture, buff colored, and very rich. It is especially good when coated with bitter chocolate.

Cold water test when candy reaches 238° F.: soft ball.

Yield (large recipe): number of pieces—thirty-six; weight —one and one-eighth pounds.

## BROWN SUGAR OPERAS

| LARGE RECIPE | SMALL RECIPE |
|---|---|
| Granulated sugar, 2 cups | Granulated sugar, 1 cup |
| Brown sugar, 2 cups | Brown sugar, 1 cup |
| Salt, ⅛ teaspoon | Salt, ¹⁄₁₆ teaspoon |
| Light corn syrup, 2 table-spoons | Light corn syrup, 1 table-spoon |
| Condensed milk, 1 cup | Condensed milk, ½ cup |
| Milk, 1½ cups | Milk, ¾ cup |
| Cream, ½ cup | Cream, ¼ cup |
| Vanilla, 1 teaspoon | Vanilla, ½ teaspoon |

Put all the ingredients, except the vanilla, into a saucepan and cook, stirring constantly, until the temperature 238° F. is reached.

Cool to 110° F. (lukewarm). Add vanilla. Beat until the candy is creamy and thick enough to hold its shape and has lost its shiny appearance. A comparatively long time is needed for this beating. Pour into slightly greased pans.

When cold cut into pieces the size of caramels.

Cold water test when candy reaches 238° F.: soft ball.

Yield (large recipe): number of pieces—seventy-two; weight—two and one-half pounds.

**General Suggestions.**—Caramels burn very easily so care must be taken in their making. Select a heavy aluminum, copper, block tin, or unchipped agate saucepan. It is better to cook over a low flame and it is necessary to stir constantly to prevent curdling and scorching.

The pans into which caramels are turned when done should be very slightly greased. Excess butter in the pans will make caramels greasy to handle. Use a square or rectangular pan, rather than a round one or a platter, so that all caramels may be of good shape.

Turn the caramels out of the pan so that they can be cut evenly. Use a large knife and cut the whole length of the block of candy with one stroke. If you find it difficult to cut "by eye," mark the candy, and follow the mark. It is quite important to have caramels well cut and neatly wrapped.

Wrapping should be done as soon after the caramels are cut as possible. Cut the paper into pieces of the right shape and size for wrapping. Do not have the paper so wide that folded ends must be brought over the top of the caramel.

## HONEY CARAMELS

| LARGE RECIPE | SMALL RECIPE |
|---|---|
| Sugar, 2 cups | Sugar, 1 cup |
| Light corn syrup, 1 cup | Light corn syrup, ½ cup |
| Condensed milk, 1 cup | Condensed milk, ½ cup |
| Cream, ½ cup | Cream, ¼ cup |
| Milk, ½ cup | Milk, ¼ cup |
| Strained honey, ½ cup | Strained honey, ¼ cup |
| Butter, ¼ cup | Butter, 2 tablespoons |
| Vanilla, 2 teaspoons | Vanilla, 1 teaspoon |

Stir together all the ingredients, except the vanilla, and cook over a low flame, stirring constantly, until the mixture reaches 248° F.

Remove from fire, add vanilla, and turn at once into a very slightly greased pan. When cold, turn the block of candy out of the pan in order to cut it more evenly. Cut into squares with a large, sharp knife.

Wrap each caramel in waxed paper.

Cold water test of caramels at 248° F.: a ball of the firmness of the caramel when cold.

Yield (large recipe): seventy-two caramels; weight—two pounds five ounces.

## VANILLA CARAMELS

| LARGE RECIPE | SMALL RECIPE |
|---|---|
| Sugar, 2 cups | Sugar, 1 cup |
| Light corn syrup, 1 cup | Light corn syrup, ½ cup |
| Condensed milk, 1 cup | Condensed milk, ½ cup |
| Cream, ½ cup | Cream, ¼ cup |
| Milk, 1 cup | Milk, ½ cup |
| Butter, ¼ cup | Butter, 2 tablespoons |
| Vanilla, 2 teaspoons | Vanilla, 1 teaspoon |

Mix together all the ingredients except the vanilla, and cook over a low flame, stirring constantly, until the mixture reaches 248° F.

Remove from fire, add vanilla, and turn at once into a very slightly greased pan. When cold, turn the block of candy out of the pan in order to cut it more evenly. Cut into squares with a large, sharp knife.

Wrap each caramel in waxed paper.

Cold water test of caramels at 246° F.: a ball of the firmness of the caramel when cold.

Yield (large recipe): seventy-two caramels; weight—two and one-fourth pounds.

## EVERYDAY VANILLA CARAMELS

| LARGE RECIPE | SMALL RECIPE |
|---|---|
| Granulated sugar, 2 cups | Granulated sugar, 1 cup |
| Brown sugar, 1 cup | Brown sugar, ½ cup |
| Light corn syrup, 1 cup | Light corn syrup, ½ cup |
| Cream, 1 cup | Cream, ½ cup |
| Milk, 2 cups | Milk, 1 cup |
| Butter, ½ cup | Butter, ¼ cup |
| Vanilla, 4 teaspoons | Vanilla, 2 teaspoons |

Put all the ingredients, except the vanilla, into a saucepan and cook, stirring constantly, over a low flame until the candy reaches the temperature 248° F.

Remove from the fire, add vanilla, and turn at once into slightly greased pans. When cold remove from the pan; cut into squares and wrap.

Cold water test when the candy reaches 248° F.: a ball of the firmness desired in the finished caramel.

Yield (large recipe): seventy-two caramels; weight—two and one-half pounds.

## MAPLE CARAMELS

| LARGE RECIPE | SMALL RECIPE |
|---|---|
| Sugar, 2 cups | Sugar, 1 cup |
| Light corn syrup, 1 cup | Light corn syrup, ½ cup |
| Condensed milk, 1 cup | Condensed milk, ½ cup |
| Cream, ½ cup | Cream, ¼ cup |
| Milk, ½ cup | Milk, ¼ cup |
| Maple syrup, 1 cup | Maple syrup, ½ cup |
| Butter, ¼ cup | Butter, 2 tablespoons |
| Vanilla, 2 teaspoons | Vanilla, 1 teaspoon |

Mix together all of the ingredients except the vanilla. Cook over a low flame, stirring constantly, until the mixture reaches 248° F.

Remove from fire, add vanilla, and turn at once into a very slightly greased pan.

When cold, turn the block of candy out of the pan in order to cut it more evenly.  Cut into squares with a large, sharp knife.

Wrap each caramel in waxed paper.

Cold water test of caramels at 248° F.: a ball of the firmness of the caramel when cold.

Yield (large recipe): seventy-two caramels; weight—two and one-fourth pounds.

## CHOCOLATE CARAMELS

| LARGE RECIPE | SMALL RECIPE |
|---|---|
| Sugar, 2 cups | Sugar, 1 cup |
| Light corn syrup, 1 cup | Light corn syrup, ½ cup |
| Condensed milk, 1 cup | Condensed milk, ½ cup |
| Cream, ½ cup | Cream, ¼ cup |
| Milk, 1 cup | Milk, ½ cup |
| Chocolate, 6 squares (6 ounces) | Chocolate, 3 squares (3 ounces) |
| Vanilla, 2 teaspoons | Vanilla, 1 teaspoon |

Chocolate should be broken into small pieces, but it need not be grated.

Stir together all of the ingredients except the vanilla and cook over a low flame, stirring constantly, until the mixture reaches 246° F.

Remove from fire, add vanilla, and turn at once into a very slightly greased pan.

When cold, turn the block of candy out of the pan in order to cut it more evenly.  Cut into squares.

Wrap each caramel in waxed paper.

Cold water test of caramels at 246° F.: a ball of the firmness of the caramel when cold.

Yield (large recipe): seventy-two caramels; weight—two and one-half pounds.

## BROWN SUGAR CARAMELS

| LARGE RECIPE | SMALL RECIPE |
|---|---|
| Brown sugar, 2 cups | Brown sugar, 1 cup |
| Granulated sugar, 1 cup | Granulated sugar, ½ cup |
| Light corn syrup, ½ cup | Light corn syrup, ¼ cup |
| Cream, 1 cup | Cream, ½ cup |
| Milk, 2 cups | Milk, 1 cup |
| Butter, ½ cup | Butter, ¼ cup |
| Vanilla, 4 teaspoons | Vanilla, 2 teaspoons |
| Nut meats, 1 cup | Nut meats, ½ cup |

Mix together all of the ingredients, except the vanilla and nut meats, and cook over a low flame, stirring constantly, until the mixture reaches 248° F.

Remove from fire, add vanilla and nut meats, and turn at once into a slightly greased pan. When cold, turn the block of candy out of the pan in order to cut it evenly. Cut into squares with a large, sharp knife.

Wrap each caramel in waxed paper.

Cold water test of caramels at 248° F.: a ball of the firmness of the caramel when finished.

Yield (large recipe): seventy-two caramels; weight—two and one-half pounds.

## CREAMY CARAMELS

| LARGE RECIPE | SMALL RECIPE |
|---|---|
| Sugar, 2 cups | Sugar, 1 cup |
| Light corn syrup, 1¼ cup | Light corn syrup, ⅝ cup |
| Milk, 2 cups | Milk, 1 cup |
| Cream, 1 cup | Cream, ½ cup |
| Butter, 2 tablespoons | Butter, 1 tablespoon |
| Fondant, 1½ cups | Fondant, ¾ cup |
| Vanilla, 2 teaspoons | Vanilla, 1 teaspoon |

Put the sugar, corn syrup, milk, and cream into a saucepan and cook until the temperature 242° F. is reached. During the cooking the mixture must be stirred quite constantly because it curdles and scorches easily. Remove from fire, add butter, and set aside to cool for about five minutes to 180° F.

Add fondant and vanilla and stir until thoroughly blended. Pour into slightly greased pans.

When cold turn the block of candy out of the pan in order to cut evenly. Cut into pieces a little less than one inch square.

The texture of this candy is a cross between that of a caramel and an opera cream, one that is seldom duplicated in commercial candy. It has excellent keeping qualities.

Cold water test when the candy reaches 242° F. soft to firm ball.

Yield (large recipe): seventy-two caramels; weight—two pounds.


## CARAMEL VARIATIONS

**Caramel Nut Roll.**—Make caramels, using small recipe, for any kind of caramel desired—vanilla, honey, chocolate, etc.

When the caramels are cooked set the saucepan into a pan of hot water, to prevent the caramel from hardening.

Make a roll of fondant or divinity about three inches long and three-fourths of an inch in diameter. Lay on a fork and dip quickly into the hot caramel mixture. Allow to stay in the caramel only long enough to be coated, or the fondant will melt.

Remove the roll from the saucepan and drop it into nut meats on waxed paper. Turn with a fork until all parts of the roll are covered. Press with the hands so that the nuts will be firmly imbedded in the roll. It is necessary to have plenty of nuts in which to drop the roll, or the caramel will stick to the waxed paper and be pulled away from the fondant.

Better results are obtained if about half the nut meats are

whole, and half broken in two or three pieces. The smaller pieces fill spaces between the whole nuts.

The caramel which is left after dipping can be poured into a slightly greased pan and cut into squares. It will become sugary because of the bits of fondant which have been washed off in the dipping, hence it should not be mixed with freshly cooked caramel.

Variety may be obtained by adding nuts, cocoanut, or nuts and cherries to the fondant center of the roll.

The center roll can be made from any kind of fondant which is firm enough to mold. Butter fondant is especially good. Opera creams, divinity, nougat, fudge, or penuchi may be used for the center roll. Or it may be made from one kind of caramel and dipped into another—as a chocolate caramel dipped into vanilla caramel.

**Nut Caramels.**—Nut caramels can be made by the addition of nuts to any of the recipes given for caramels. Add one and one-half cups of nuts to the large recipe.

The nuts should be cut or broken into fairly large pieces. If chopped there will be a fine powder which will cloud the candy.

If pecans or English walnuts are to be used, they should be freshened in the oven. Black walnuts or Brazil nuts are especially good in caramels.

**Layer Caramels.**—Layer caramels add a great deal to the appearance of a box of candy. These may be made in two or three layers, of different kinds of caramels, or of caramels combined with nougat or divinity.

A layer of light colored caramel, capped by a layer of dark chocolate caramel, makes a candy both good-looking and delicious.

Layer caramels are made by pouring a thin layer into a pan, allowing it to cool, and then pouring in a second layer of contrasting color and flavor.

The three-layer caramels may be made with caramel top and bottom and nougat or divinity between.

If to be used at once, butter fondant can be combined with caramels to form layer candies.  However, it should not be used if to be kept, because the fondant dries out more quickly than the caramels and the layers will separate.

# Chapter 9:

## DIVINITY AND NOUGAT

**General Directions for Divinity.**—Generally, divinity is served in rough, irregular pieces dropped from a spoon on waxed paper.

However, the divinity may be poured into a pan and cut into squares. If done in this way it has better keeping qualities, is more moist, and has a more attractive appearance than when dropped.

If, during the cooking of the syrup, sugar crystals form on the side of the pan, they may be washed away by using a piece of wet cheesecloth wrapped around the tines of a fork.

While divinity is cooking, break the eggs and have whites ready to use. Begin beating the egg whites when candy is almost cooked so that the syrup will not have opportunity to cool. Beat eggs until stiff, add the hot syrup gradually, beating during the addition.

The first portion of the syrup may become hard when it comes in contact with the cold egg white, but as more syrup is added the heat will soften it and it can be beaten into the mixture.

A wire whisk is easier to use for beating in the syrup than a rotary beater because, as the mixture stiffens, it becomes too heavy for the rotary beater.

If possible arrange to have two persons work on the combining of the syrup and the egg whites, as this step is much easier if one can pour while the other beats. This combining is more difficult than the making of frosting because the syrup has been cooked to a higher temperature and is more prone to harden.

When the candy is being dropped from the spoon, the work must be done quickly or the candy will become too hard.

If for some reason the divinity does not harden, cook it over hot water until a small portion dropped on waxed paper becomes firm.

Recipes of only one size have been given for some kinds of divinity. If too large a recipe is used, the beating is difficult. If the quantities used are too small, the syrup is apt to harden before it can be combined with the egg whites.

## DOUBLE DIVINITY

| LARGE RECIPE | SMALL RECIPE |
|---|---|
| *Mixture One* | *Mixture One* |
| Sugar, 3 cups | Sugar, 1½ cups |
| Water, ¾ cup | Water, ½ cup |
| Light corn syrup, 1 cup | Light corn syrup, ½ cup |
| *Mixture Two* | *Mixture Two* |
| Sugar, 1 cup | Sugar, 1 cup |
| Water, ½ cup | Water, ½ cup |
| Egg whites, 3 | Egg whites, 2 |
| Vanilla, 1 teaspoon | Vanilla, ½ teaspoon |
| Nut meats, 1 cup | Nut meats, ⅔ cup |

Cook Mixture One in a saucepan, stirring until the sugar is dissolved; then cook, without stirring, until the temperature 246° F. is reached.

While Mixture One is cooking, get Mixture Two (sugar and water) ready, and as soon as Mixture One is cooked put Mixture Two on the fire.

Remove Mixture One from the fire and pour it slowly over the beaten egg whites, beating constantly during the addition. Continue beating until Mixture Two has reached the temperature 255° F. Pour this hot syrup into the first mixture and beat until the candy will not adhere to the finger when the surface is gently touched. Add the vanilla and nut meats and spread in a slightly buttered pan.

Cut in squares when cold.

This recipe is more trouble to make than the simpler recipe for divinity, but the candy is softer and creamier.

Cold water test for Mixture One when 246° F. is reached: firm ball.

Cold water test for Mixture Two when 255° F. is reached: very firm ball.

Yield (large recipe): number of pieces—seventy-two; weight —three pounds.

## HONEY ALMOND DIVINITY

| LARGE RECIPE | SMALL RECIPE |
|---|---|
| *Mixture One* | *Mixture One* |
| Sugar, 3 cups | Sugar, 1½ cups |
| Water, ¾ cup | Water, ½ cup |
| Light corn syrup, ½ cup | Light corn syrup, ¼ cup |
| Strained honey, ½ cup | Strained honey, ¼ cup |
| *Mixture Two* | *Mixture Two* |
| Sugar, 1 cup | Sugar, 1 cup |
| Water, ½ cup | Water, ½ cup |
| Egg whites, 3 | Egg whites, 2 |
| Vanilla, 1 teaspoon | Vanilla, ½ teaspoon |
| Almonds, 1½ cups | Almonds, 1 cup |

Blanch the almonds, shred them coarsely, and brown them in a slow oven.

Cook Mixture One in a saucepan, stirring until the sugar is dissolved; then cook, without stirring, until the temperature 246° F. is reached.

While Mixture One is cooking get Mixture Two (sugar and water) ready, and as soon as Mixture One is cooked put Mixture Two on the fire.

Remove Mixture One from the fire and pour it slowly over the beaten egg whites, beating constantly during the addition. Continue beating until Mixture Two has reached the temperature 255° F.  Pour this hot syrup into the first mixture and beat until the candy will not adhere to the finger when the surface is gently touched. Add the vanilla and nut meats and spread in a slightly buttered pan.

Cut in squares when cold.

Cold water test for Mixture One when 246° F. is reached: firm ball.

Cold water test for Mixture Two when 255° F. is reached: very firm ball.

Yield (large recipe): number of pieces—seventy-two; weight—three pounds.

## VANILLA DIVINITY

> Sugar, 2⅓ cups
> Light corn syrup, ⅔ cup
> Water, ½ cup
> Salt, ¼ teaspoon
> Egg whites, 2
> Vanilla, ½ teaspoon
> Nut meats, 1 cup (pecans or walnuts)

Put the sugar, corn syrup, salt, and water into a saucepan and cook, stirring until the sugar is completely dissolved. Continue cooking, without stirring, until the temperature 265° F. is reached.

Remove from the fire and gradually pour the syrup over the egg whites, which have been beaten until stiff during the latter part of the cooking of the syrup. Beat during this addition. Continue beating until the candy will hold its shape when dropped from the spoon. Add vanilla and nut meats; mix thoroughly.

Drop by teaspoonfuls on waxed paper or turn into a slightly greased pan and cut into squares.

Cold water test of syrup when it reaches 265° F.: hard, almost brittle.

Yield: number of pieces—twenty to twenty-four (size of a walnut); weight—one and one-fourth pounds.

## MAPLE DIVINITY

Sugar, 2⅓ cups
Maple syrup, ½ cup
Light corn syrup, ⅔ cup
Water, ¼ cup
Salt, ¼ teaspoon
Egg whites, 2
Nut meats, 1 cup (pecans or walnuts)
Vanilla, ½ teaspoon

Put the sugar, maple syrup, corn syrup, salt, and water into a saucepan and cook, stirring until the sugar is completely dissolved. Continue cooking, without stirring, until the temperature 265° F. is reached.

Remove from the fire and gradually pour the syrup over the egg whites, which have been beaten until stiff during the latter part of the cooking of the syrup. Work quickly, beating during this addition.

Continue beating until the divinity will hold its shape when dropped from the spoon. Add nuts and vanilla and mix.

Drop by teaspoonfuls on waxed paper or turn into a very slightly greased pan and cut into squares.

Cold water test of syrup when it reaches 265° F.: hard, almost brittle.

Yield: number of pieces—twenty to twenty-six (size of a walnut); weight—one and one-fourth pounds.

## BROWN SUGAR DIVINITY

Brown sugar, 1 cup
Granulated sugar, 1 cup
Light corn syrup, ⅓ cup
Water, ½ cup
Salt, ¼ teaspoon
Egg whites, 2
Nut meats, 1 cup (pecans or walnuts)
Vanilla, ½ teaspoon

Put the brown sugar, granulated sugar, corn syrup, salt, and water into a saucepan and cook, stirring until the sugar is completely dissolved. Continue cooking, without stirring, until the temperature 267° F. is reached. (This temperature is higher than that given for the white divinity because the brown sugar tends to make the candy more sticky.)

Remove from the fire and gradually pour the syrup over the egg whites, which have been beaten until stiff during the latter part of the cooking of the syrup. Beat during this addition.

Continue beating until the divinity will hold its shape when dropped from the spoon. Add vanilla and nut meats. Mix thoroughly.

Drop by teaspoonfuls on waxed paper or turn into a slightly greased pan and cut into squares.

Cold water test of syrup when it reaches 267° F.: hard, almost brittle.

Yield: number of pieces—twenty (size of a walnut); weight —one pound.

## CHOCOLATE DIVINITY

> Sugar, 2⅓ cups
> Light corn syrup, ⅔ cup
> Water, ½ cup
> Salt, ¼ teaspoon
> Egg whites, 2
> Cocoa, ⅓ cup
> Nut meats, 1 cup (pecans or walnuts)
> Vanilla, ½ teaspoon

Put the sugar, corn syrup, salt, and water into a saucepan and cook, stirring until the sugar is completely dissolved. Continue cooking, without stirring, until the temperature 265° F. is reached.

Remove from the fire and gradually pour the syrup over the egg whites, which have been beaten until stiff during the latter part of the cooking of the syrup.  Beat during this addition.  Add cocoa and beat until the candy will hold its shape when dropped from the spoon.  Add vanilla and nut meats and mix thoroughly.

Drop by teaspoonfuls on waxed paper or turn into a slightly greased pan and cut into squares.

Cold water test of syrup when it reaches 265° F.: hard, almost brittle.

Yield: number of pieces—twenty to twenty-four (size of a walnut); weight—one and one-fourth pounds.

## CHERRY DIVINITY

> **Sugar, 2½ cups**
> **Light corn syrup, ⅔ cup**
> **Water, ½ cup**
> **Salt, ¼ teaspoon**
> **Egg whites, 2**
> **Vanilla, ½ teaspoon**
> **Candied cherries, 1 cup**

Slice the candied cherries.

Put the sugar, syrup, salt, and water into a saucepan and cook, stirring until the sugar is completely dissolved.  Continue the cooking, without stirring, until the temperature 265° F. is reached.

Remove from the fire and gradually pour the syrup over the egg whites which have been beaten stiff during the latter part of the cooking of the syrup.  Beat during this addition.  Continue beating until the candy will hold its shape when dropped from the spoon.  Add vanilla and cherries.

Drop by teaspoonfuls on waxed paper or turn into a slightly greased pan and cut into squares.

Cold water test of syrup when it reaches 265° F.: hard, almost brittle.

Yield: number of pieces—twenty-six (size of a walnut); weight—one and one-third pounds.

## DIVINITY COMBINATIONS

**Divinity Rolls.**—Double divinity is best adapted for this recipe, as it is somewhat more pliable than the plain divinity and hence can be shaped as a roll more easily. Dip the roll in caramel according to the general directions given under caramel nut rolls. Use the same kind of nuts for the outside of the roll as are used in the divinity.

**Divinity Double Decker.**—Into a medium sized, slightly greased pan pour a layer of divinity a little less than one-half inch thick. On this place a layer of dark fudge, caramels, penuchi, or maple creams. Allow to stand until firm. Remove the block of candy from the pan and cut into squares. Wrap in waxed paper.

**Divinity "Layer Cake."**—Into a medium sized, slightly greased pan pour a layer of double divinity about three-fourths of an inch thick. When firm, turn the block of candy from the pan and cut into halves. Spread the top of one piece with melted coating chocolate, lay the second piece on top of this, and frost the sides and top with the coating chocolate. Sprinkle with chopped nuts, if desired. When cold cut in slices as layer cake.

**Cocoanut Divinity.**—Either fresh or desiccated cocoanut may be added to give more flavor to the divinity. Spread the cocoanut in a thin sheet on a pan and heat in the oven until delicately browned. This develops flavor and removes excess moisture from the fresh cocoanut. Add three-fourths cup of cocoanut to each recipe of divinity.

## SEAFOAM

| | |
|---|---|
| Brown sugar, 3 cups | Egg whites, 2 |
| Water, ¾ cup | Vanilla, 1 teaspoon |
| Salt, ¼ teaspoon | |

Cook sugar, water, and salt together, stirring until the sugar is dissolved. Continue cooking, without stirring, until the syrup reaches the temperature 255° F.

Remove from the fire and gradually pour it over the egg whites, which have been beaten until stiff during the latter part of the cooking of the syrup. Beat while pouring. Continue beating until the candy cools somewhat, and will hold its shape when dropped from the spoon. Add vanilla.

Drop by teaspoonfuls on waxed paper.

Nuts may be added just before the candy is dropped.

Cold water test when the syrup reaches 255° F.: hard—but not brittle.

Yield: number of pieces—twenty (size of walnut); weight—three-fourths of a pound.

## NOUGAT

**General Directions for Nougat.**—In a box of assorted bonbons nougat is one of the most popular candies—yet it is seldom made at home. However, it is not too difficult for the amateur candy maker, and although it takes a long time to prepare the almonds and pistachio nuts the results are worth the trouble.

Real nougat always contains honey, almonds, and pistachio nuts. It is covered top and bottom with nougat wafers. These are Japanese rice wafers and can be purchased in large sheets from wholesale confectioners. They are similar to those used to feed gold fish and if you cannot secure the regular nougat wafers these smaller sheets of rice wafers can be used.

The recipe given here makes a nougat that will not be brittle. It will be firm enough to hold its shape and should not be sticky. The recipe may seem to have too many nuts when these are first added, but they can be beaten in and the nuts help to make the candy good. The flavor is greatly improved if the almonds are browned after being blanched and shredded.

The conventional shape for nougat is rectangular and the pieces should be about an inch and a half long, half an inch wide, and from one-half to three-fourths of an inch thick.

Nougat must be wrapped as soon as it is cut, as exposure to the air makes it sticky.

It has splendid keeping qualities and can be made in advance for packing Christmas boxes.

## NOUGAT

Sugar, 1 cup
Water, ½ cup
Strained honey, ½ cup
Light corn syrup, 3 tablespoons
Egg whites, 2
Almonds, 2½ cups
Pistachio nuts, ½ cup
Vanilla, 1 teaspoon

Blanch the almonds and pistachio nuts and shred them coarsely. Brown the almonds slightly in a slow oven. If the pistachio nuts are browned their color will become dull.

Cook the sugar, water, and one-half of the corn syrup together, stirring until the sugar is dissolved. Continue cooking to the temperature 290° F. Remove from the fire.

During the last few minutes of cooking the syrup, beat the egg whites until stiff. Add the hot syrup gradually to the egg whites, beating during the addition.

While adding the first syrup to the egg whites, begin cooking the honey and the remainder of the corn syrup together. Continue this cooking until the temperature 290° F. is reached. Remove from the fire and add at once to the egg white mixture, pouring it in gradually and beating while adding.

Add nuts and cook over hot water until the mixture dries, stirring while cooking. Test the candy by taking a small amount out in a spoon. When it holds its shape when cold and is not sticky to the touch, it is done.

Add vanilla, pour into pans which have been lined with nougat wafers, and cover with nougat wafers. Place a pan, board, or other smooth surface over the top of the candy and press with a heavy weight for twelve hours or longer.

Remove the block of candy from the pan and cut into rectangular pieces. Wrap each piece in waxed paper.

Cold water test of syrup when it reaches 290° F.: brittle.

Yield: number of pieces—forty-eight; weight—one and three-fourths pounds.

## NOUGAT COMBINATIONS

**Nougat Double Decker.**—Line the bottom of a pan with nougat wafers and pour in nougat, making a layer a little less than one-half inch thick. Do not cover this with nougat wafers, but directly on top pour a layer of caramel candy which is almost cold. Hot caramel will melt the nougat. Any kind of caramels may be used, but the darker ones, such as chocolate or brown sugar, will give inviting color contrasts.

Nougat should be combined only with candy similar to it in consistency, as caramels. A cream candy, such as fondant or fudge, would dry out and the layers would separate.

**Nougat Rolls.**—Cool the nougat, shape it into a roll, and dip it in caramel according to the general directions given under caramel nut rolls. The roll should be covered with browned chopped almonds instead of pecans.

**Nougat Caramel Sandwiches.**—A thin layer of nougat can be placed between two thin layers of caramels and the candy cut into squares to form the sandwich caramels which are so well liked.

**General Directions for Taffies.**—Use a large sized saucepan in cooking molasses taffy in order to allow plenty of room for the molasses to "boil up." In no other candy is there so much danger of "boiling over."

Molasses burns easily, therefore the taffy should be cooked slowly during the last few minutes in order to prevent scorching.

Taffy is ready to be pulled when the edges begin to stiffen and the mass can be handled. Do not allow it to become too cool or it will be too hard to pull. If taffy should become too hard to pull, it can be softened by placing it in a moderate oven for a few minutes.

Do not grease the hands for pulling taffy. The fingers may be dipped into cornstarch, but even this is not necessary.

When pulling taffy use the thumb and fingers, rather than the whole hand. With this method there is less danger of having the candy stick to the hands and the taffy is more fluffy.

Pull taffy until cold, so that the pieces will hold their shape after they are cut.

Use scissors for cutting into pieces of the desired size. This is much quicker than using a knife.

To make pieces of an attractive shape, stretch the taffy out into a rope, cut off one piece, turn the rope half over, and cut another piece about an inch long. Continue the turning after each cutting. Keep the pieces separated after cutting.

If taffy is to be kept the pieces should be wrapped in waxed paper as soon as cut.

It is customary to cut the papers long enough to allow for twisting the ends.

If taffy is to be served at once, lay the pieces on a buttered plate, keeping them separated so they will not stick together.

If taffy sugars it can be recooked. Put candy into a saucepan with two tablespoons of corn syrup and three-fourths of a cup of water. Heat slowly at first, until taffy is dissolved. Then cook according to directions given in recipe.

## MOLASSES TAFFY

| LARGE RECIPE | SMALL RECIPE |
|---|---|
| Granulated sugar, 1 cup | Granulated sugar, ½ cup |
| Brown sugar, 1 cup | Brown sugar, ½ cup |
| Light molasses, 2 cups | Light molasses, 1 cup |
| Water, ¾ cup | Water, ½ cup |
| Butter, ¼ cup | Butter, 2 tablespoons |
| Soda, ⅛ teaspoon | Soda, $\frac{1}{16}$ teaspoon |
| Salt, ¼ teaspoon | Salt, ⅛ teaspoon |

Put the sugars, molasses, and water into a saucepan and cook to the temperature 265° F. It will be necessary to cook the candy slowly and to stir it during the latter part of the cooking in order to prevent burning.

Remove from the fire, add the butter, soda, and salt and stir just enough to mix well. In adding the soda be sure it is free from lumps. Turn into a greased pan and allow to stand until cool enough to handle.

Gather into a ball and pull until rather firm and of a light yellow color. Stretch out in a long rope. Cut into pieces. If not to be used at once, wrap in waxed paper.

Cold water test when candy reaches 265° F.: hard but not quite brittle.

Yield (large recipe): number of pieces—seventy (about one inch long); weight—one and three-fourths pounds.

## MOLASSES MINT TAFFY

| LARGE RECIPE | SMALL RECIPE |
|---|---|
| Molasses, 2 cups | Molasses, 1 cup |
| Vinegar, 2 teaspoons | Vinegar, 1 teaspoon |
| Butter, 2 tablespoons | Butter, 1 tablespoon |
| Salt, ⅛ teaspoon | Salt, $\frac{1}{16}$ teaspoon |
| Soda, ½ teaspoon | Soda, ¼ teaspoon |
| Oil of peppermint, 6 drops | Oil of peppermint, 3 drops |

Put the molasses and vinegar into a saucepan and boil until the temperature 270° F. is reached. It will be necessary to cook the candy slowly and to stir during the latter part of the cooking to prevent burning.

Remove from the fire, add the butter, salt, and soda, taking care that the soda is free from lumps. Stir until the candy ceases to foam. Pour into a greased pan.

When cool enough to pull, pour the oil of peppermint into the center of the mass, gather the corners toward the center so that the flavoring will not be lost, remove from the pan, and pull. When the candy becomes light in color and rather firm, stretch out in a long rope, twist, and cut into small pieces.

If the candy is to be kept the pieces should be wrapped in waxed paper.

If taffy is to be served at once, lay the pieces on a buttered plate, keeping them separated so they will not stick together.

This is a hard, brittle taffy. If a softer taffy is desired, cook to 266° F.

Since no sugar is used in the recipe, the finished candy will have the flavor of the molasses. For a delicate flavor use the light-colored molasses, which is not so strong as the dark.

Cold water test when candy reaches 270° F.: hard, almost brittle.

Yield (large recipe): number of pieces—fifty (about one inch long); weight—1 pound.

## WHITE TAFFY

LARGE RECIPE

Sugar, 2 cups
Light corn syrup, ½ cup
Water, ⅔ cup
Vanilla, 1 teaspoon

SMALL RECIPE

Sugar, 1 cup
Light corn syrup, ¼ cup
Water, ½ cup
Vanilla, ½ teaspoon

Put all of the ingredients except the vanilla into a saucepan and cook, stirring until the sugar is dissolved. Continue cooking, without stirring, until the temperature 268° F. is reached. Remove from the fire and pour into greased pans.

When cool enough to handle, pour the vanilla into the center of the mass. Gather the corners toward the center so that the flavoring will not be lost. Remove from the pan and pull.

When the candy is white and rather firm, stretch out in a long rope and cut into pieces of the desired size, using scissors. If this candy is to be kept, it should be wrapped in waxed paper.

If you are giving a taffy pull for the children, divide the candy into several portions for pulling, omitting the vanilla. Add coloring to each portion, and pull it through the taffy. Use a different color for each, and add a flavor to suit the color, as wintergreen to the delicate pink, spearmint to pale green, lemon to the yellow, and peppermint to the white. Use flavoring oils instead of essences, as these are stronger and will not make the taffy sticky.

Children are always interested in striped candies. To make these, combine two batches with colors which go well together but with the same flavoring. Pull each separately until almost ready to cut and then pull them together, twisting as you pull.

Cold water test when candy reaches 268° F.: firm, nearly brittle.

Yield (large recipe): number of pieces—sixty (about one inch long); weight—one and one-eighth pounds.

## PULLED MINTS

<table>
<tr><td>LARGE RECIPE</td><td>SMALL RECIPE</td></tr>
<tr><td>Sugar, 3 cups</td><td>Sugar, 1½ cups</td></tr>
<tr><td>Water, 1 cup</td><td>Water, ¾ cup</td></tr>
<tr><td>Corn syrup, 2 tablespoons</td><td>Corn syrup, 1 tablespoon</td></tr>
<tr><td>Oil of peppermint, 10 drops</td><td>Oil of peppermint, 5 drops</td></tr>
</table>

Put all of the ingredients except the oil of peppermint into a saucepan and cook, stirring constantly until the sugar is dissolved. Then cover and cook for two minutes so that the steam may wash down any sugar crystals from the sides of the saucepan. Remove the cover and cook, without stirring, to the temperature 265° F. During this cooking wash the sides of the saucepan occasionally with a piece of wet cheese-cloth to remove sugar crystals.

Remove from the fire and pour into a greased pan. When cool enough to handle put the oil of peppermint into the center of the mass, fold over the corners, so that the peppermint will not be lost and gradually gather the candy into a ball and pull. It will soon become white and fluffy. Pull it until it becomes quite firm.

Stretch out in a long rope and cut into *small* pieces.
Sift together:

**2 cups powdered sugar
1 cup cornstarch**

Spread this mixture over the bottom of a shallow pan in a layer about one-fourth of an inch thick.

Drop the pieces of candy into this pan, keeping them separated. Cover with a second layer of the cornstarch and sugar, and put aside in a warm place (as a warming oven, with the door left open) over night or until they become "creamy."

Sift off the sugar and cornstarch from the mints and pack them away in covered jars or tin boxes. Keep two days or longer before using. As the mints are kept they "ripen," becoming more creamy.

The sugar and cornstarch can be saved and used when mints are made again.

Suggestions: oil of wintergreen may be used instead of oil of peppermint and the candy colored pink, or oil of spearmint and a green color may be used.

Cold water test when candy reaches 265° F.: hard, almost brittle.

Yield (large recipe): number of pieces—one hundred and twenty (one-half inch long); weight of candy—one and one-half pounds.

## SEA SIDE TAFFY

| LARGE RECIPE | SMALL RECIPE |
|---|---|
| Sugar, 2 cups | Sugar, 1 cup |
| Light corn syrup, 1 cup | Light corn syrup, ½ cup |
| Water, 1 cup | Water, ½ cup |
| Salt, 1½ teaspoons | Salt, ¾ teaspoon |
| Glycerine, 2 teaspoons | Glycerine, 1 teaspoon |
| Butter, 1 tablespoon | Butter, ½ tablespoon |
| Vanilla, 2 teaspoons | Vanilla, 1 teaspoon |

Put all of the ingredients except the butter and flavoring into a saucepan and cook, stirring until the sugar is dissolved.

If sugar crystals form on the sides of the saucepan during cooking, wash them away with a piece of wet cheesecloth.

Continue cooking until the temperature 262° F. is reached. Remove from fire, add butter, and when butter is melted pour into a greased pan.

When cool enough to handle gather into a ball and pull until it is rather firm.  Add flavoring while pulling.  Stretch out in a long rope and cut into pieces of the desired size. Usually the pieces of sea side taffies are about two inches in length.

Wrap in waxed paper.

Sea side taffies can be colored during the pulling.  The coloring paste can be added to the taffy and pulled through it.

Different flavors can be added to suit the colors. The pink taffy is usually flavored with wintergreen; white, vanilla; green, spearmint; etc. If coloring paste is used, dissolve it in as little water as possible.

Cold water test when candy reaches 262° F.: firm, almost brittle.

Yield (large recipe): number of pieces—sixty (about two inches in length); weight—one and one-third pounds.

## CHOCOLATE TAFFY

| LARGE RECIPE | SMALL RECIPE |
|---|---|
| Sugar, 2 cups | Sugar, 1 cup |
| Light corn syrup, ½ cup | Light corn syrup, ¼ cup |
| Water, ½ cup | Water, ¼ cup |
| Chocolate, 3 squares (3 ounces) | Chocolate, 1½ squares (1½ ounces) |
| Vanilla, 1 teaspoon | Vanilla, ½ teaspoon |

Put all of the ingredients except the vanilla into a saucepan and cook to the temperature 260° F. It will be necessary to cook the candy slowly and to stir it during the latter part of the cooking in order to prevent burning.

Remove from the fire and pour into a greased pan. When cool enough to handle pour the vanilla into the center of the mass. Gather the corners toward the center so that the flavoring will not be lost, remove from the pan and pull. When it is light brown and rather firm, stretch out in a long rope and cut into pieces of the desired size.

If this candy is to be kept it should be wrapped in waxed paper. If it is to be served at once, lay the pieces on a buttered plate, keeping them separated so that they will not stick together.

Cold water test when candy reaches 260° F.: hard but not brittle.

Yield (large recipe): number of pieces—sixty (about one inch long); weight—one and one-fourth pounds.

## HONEY TAFFY

LARGE RECIPE

Sugar, 2 cups
Strained honey, ¾ cup
Water, 1 cup
Butter, 2 tablespoons

SMALL RECIPE

Sugar, 1 cup
Strained honey, ⅜ cup
Water, ⅔ cup
Butter, 1 tablespoon

Measure the honey carefully as an excess will make the candy too soft and sticky.

Put the sugar, honey, and water into a saucepan and cook, stirring until the sugar is dissolved.. Continue cooking, stirring occasionally to prevent burning, until the temperature 278° F. is reached. Add butter and stir only enough to mix. Pour into greased pans and allow to stand until cool enough to handle.

Gather into a ball and pull until rather firm and light in color. Stretch out in a long rope. Cut into pieces with the scissors. Wrap in waxed paper. This is a rather soft taffy.

Cold water test when the candy reaches 278° F.: hard but not quite brittle.

Yield (large recipe): number of pieces—seventy; weight— one and one-fourth pounds.

## CHOCOLATE SEA SIDE TAFFY

LARGE RECIPE

Sugar, 2 cups
Light corn syrup, 1 cup
Water, 1 cup
Salt, 1½ teaspoons
Glycerine, 2 teaspoons
Butter, 1 tablespoon
Chocolate, 4 squares
  (4 ounces)
Vanilla, 1 teaspoon

SMALL RECIPE

Sugar, 1 cup
Light corn syrup, ½ cup
Water, ½ cup
Salt, ¾ teaspoon
Glycerine, 1 teaspoon
Butter, ½ tablespoon
Chocolate, 2 squares
  (2 ounces)
Vanilla, ½ teaspoon

Put the chocolate over warm water to melt. Add the butter.

Put all of the other ingredients except the vanilla into a saucepan and cook, stirring until the sugar is dissolved.

Continue cooking until the temperature 264° F. is reached. Remove from fire, add butter and melted chocolate, and stir only enough to mix.  Pour into a greased pan.

When cool enough to handle pour the vanilla into the center of the mass.  Gather the corners toward the center so that the flavoring will not be lost, remove from the pan, and pull.  The pulling is rather difficult at first because the chocolate has not entirely combined with the syrup.  After a few minutes' pulling, it has worked through the mass.

When the candy is rather firm, stretch out in a long rope and cut into pieces of the desired size.  Usually the pieces of this taffy are about two inches in length.

Wrap in waxed paper.

Cold water test when candy reaches 264° F.: firm, almost brittle.

Yield (large recipe): number of pieces—sixty-six (about two inches in length); weight—one and two-thirds pounds.

## CREAM TAFFY

| LARGE RECIPE | SMALL RECIPE |
|---|---|
| Sugar, 2 cups | Sugar, 1 cup |
| Light corn syrup, ¼ cup | Light corn syrup, 2 tablespoons |
| Water, ¾ cup | Water, ½ cup |
| Cream, 1 cup | Cream, ½ cup |
| Vanilla, 1 teaspoon | Vanilla, ½ teaspoon |

Put sugar, corn syrup, and water into a saucepan and cook, stirring until the sugar is dissolved.  Continue cooking until the temperature 250° F. is reached.

Add cream and cook slowly, stirring constantly to prevent burning, until the temperature 260° F. is reached.  Remove from fire and pour into a greased pan.

When cool enough to handle pour the vanilla into the center of the mass. Gather the corners toward the center so that the flavoring will not be lost, remove from pan, and pull. When rather firm and of a light buff color stretch out in a long rope. Cut into pieces. If not to be used at once, wrap in waxed paper.

This candy is more porous than the other taffies. It has a slight caramel flavor.

Cold water test when candy reaches 250° F.: hard ball.

Cold water test when candy reaches 260° F.: harder than at 250° F.—not quite brittle.

Yield (large recipe): number of pieces—one hundred and twenty (one inch long); weight—one pound three ounces.

## MOLASSES KISSES

| LARGE RECIPE | SMALL RECIPE |
|---|---|
| Molasses, 1 cup | Molasses, ½ cup |
| Brown sugar, 1 cup | Brown sugar, ½ cup |
| Water, ½ cup | Water, ⅓ cup |
| Butter, ¼ cup | Butter, 2 tablespoons |
| Soda, ⅛ teaspoon | Soda, $\frac{1}{16}$ teaspoon |
| Oil of lemon, 4 drops | Oil of lemon, 2 drops |

Molasses kisses can be flavored with vanilla, oil of peppermint, or oil of lemon. The lemon flavoring is especially good.

Put the molasses, sugar, and water into a saucepan and cook, stirring until the sugar is dissolved. Continue the cooking, stirring enough to prevent burning, until the temperature 256° F. is reached.

Remove from fire, add butter and soda, and stir only enough to mix well. In adding the soda be sure it is free from lumps.

Pour the candy into a greased pan. When cool enough to handle pour the oil of lemon into the center of the mass. Gather the corners toward the center so that the flavoring will not be lost, remove from pan, and pull. When rather firm and light in color, stretch out in a rope about three-fourths of an inch in diameter. Flatten with a rolling pin and cut into pieces about one inch in length.

Wrap in waxed paper.

Cold water test when candy reaches 256° F.: hard ball.

Yield (large recipe): number of pieces—fifty; weight—one pound.

## CREAM KISSES

| LARGE RECIPE | SMALL RECIPE |
|---|---|
| Sugar, 2 cups | Sugar, 1 cup |
| Light corn syrup, ¾ cup | Light corn syrup, ⅓ cup |
| Cream or top milk, ½ cup | Cream or top milk, ¼ cup |
| Butter, 3 tablespoons | Butter, 1½ tablespoons |
| Flour, 2 teaspoons | Flour, 1 teaspoon |
| Water, 2 tablespoons | Water, 1 tablespoon |
| Vanilla, 2 teaspoons | Vanilla, 1 teaspoon |

Put the sugar, corn syrup, and cream into a saucepan and cook, stirring until the sugar is dissolved. Continue cooking and stirring until the temperature 256° F. is reached.

Remove from fire. Add the flour and water, which have been mixed to a paste. Stir thoroughly and cook until the temperature 256° F. is reached again. Add butter. Pour into a greased pan.

When cool enough to handle pour the vanilla into the center of the mass, gather the corners toward the center so that the flavoring will not be lost. Remove from pan and pull. When rather firm and light in color, stretch out in a rope about three-fourths of an inch in diameter. Flatten slightly with a rolling pin. Cut into pieces about one inch in length.

Wrap in waxed paper.

Cold water test when candy reaches 256° F.: hard ball.

Yield (large recipe): number of pieces—sixty; weight—one and one-fourth pounds.

# Chapter 11:

## BRITTLES, BUTTERSCOTCH, AND TOFFEES

**General Directions for Brittles.**—A brittle is just what its name implies. It is pulled out in a thin sheet and is very crisp. It is usually broken into pieces of irregular shape.

The brittle should be stirred as little as possible during cooking so that there will be no chance for crystallization of sugar. Sugar crystals should be washed from the sides of the saucepan during the candy cooking, as their presence may cause the brittle to sugar.

When adding the nuts or cocoanut mix quickly in order to avoid stirring and cooling of the candy. It is better to have the nuts or cocoanut warm when adding to the candy, because if the syrup is cooled it cannot be poured in a thin sheet. Putting the nuts or cocoanut into the oven for a few minutes also improves their flavor. Nuts should be broken or cut into small pieces when used in a brittle. When nuts are chopped there is a fine powder which clouds the brittle.

The brittle should be poured on a greased slab, or, if there is no slab, on a large, inverted, greased pan. It should not be poured into a pan, as then it cannot be stretched to a thin sheet.

To stretch a brittle pour it as quickly as possible on the greased slab or pan, press out with a spatula, and as soon as it can be touched, lift the edges and pull gently, stretching the mass out until it becomes very thin. If the quantity is large it may be necessary to break off the pieces around the edges, in order to pull the center.

If the brittle becomes sugary it can be recooked. Put it into a saucepan with three-fourths of a cup of hot water and two tablespoons of corn syrup. Heat slowly until brittle is

**77**

dissolved. Cook to temperature called for in recipe. Many brittles become sticky on standing and should therefore be used the day they are made.

## NUT BRITTLE

| LARGE RECIPE | SMALL RECIPE |
|---|---|
| Granulated sugar, 2 cups | Granulated sugar, 1 cup |
| Brown sugar, 1 cup | Brown sugar, ½ cup |
| Light corn syrup, ½ cup | Light corn syrup, ¼ cup |
| Water, ½ cup | Water, ⅓ cup |
| Butter, ¼ cup | Butter, 2 tablespoons |
| Soda, ⅛ teaspoon | Soda, $\frac{1}{16}$ teaspoon |
| Salt, ⅛ teaspoon | Salt, $\frac{1}{16}$ teaspoon |
| Nut meats, 1½ cups (broken in pieces) | Nut meats, ¾ cup (broken in pieces) |

Put the sugars, corn syrup, and water into a saucepan and cook, stirring until the sugar is dissolved. Continue cooking, without stirring, until the temperature 300° F. is reached.

Remove from fire, add salt, soda (free from lumps), and butter and stir only enough to mix well. If much stirring is done the brittle will sugar. Add nut meats and turn at once on a greased slab or on a greased inverted pan or baking sheet. Do not scrape the saucepan, as this may cause the brittle to sugar. Have enough pans to give space for the brittle to be poured out in very thin sheets.

Smooth out with a spatula. After about a half minute take hold of the edges of the candy and lifting it slightly from the slab, pull it as thin as possible. If the candy is in a large sheet it may be necessary to cut off the thin pieces at the edges in order to pull the center. Break into irregular pieces.

Peanuts or any nuts desired may be used. The nuts should be broken into small pieces.

Cold water test when candy reaches 300° F.: very brittle.

Yield (large recipe): number of pieces—eighty; weight—two pounds.

## PEANUT MOLASSES BRITTLE

Sugar, 2 cups                    Butter, ⅓ cup
Molasses, ½ cup                  Soda, 1 teaspoon
Water, ½ cup                     Peanuts, 2 cups

Put the sugar, molasses and water into a saucepan and cook, stirring until the sugar is dissolved. Continue cooking very slowly until the temperature 300° F. is reached.

Remove from the fire, stir in the butter and then beat in the soda. Add the peanuts and mix them in well. The peanuts should be blanched and roasted. If they have been salted remove excess salt before adding them to the candy. Pour out on a well greased slab or baking sheet. Smooth out with a spatula, pulling out into a thin sheet, if desired. If not, mark into squares. In any case loosen the candy from the baking sheet while it is still warm. When cold break into squares or into irregular pieces.

Cold water test when candy reaches 300° F.: very brittle.

Yield: weight—one and three-fourths pounds.

## NUT PATTIES

| LARGE RECIPE | SMALL RECIPE |
|---|---|
| Granulated sugar, 2 cups | Granulated sugar, 1 cup |
| Brown sugar, 1 cup | Brown sugar, ½ cup |
| Light corn syrup, ½ cup | Light corn syrup, ¼ cup |
| Water, ½ cup | Water, ⅓ cup |
| Butter, ¼ cup | Butter, 2 tablespoons |
| Salt, ¼ teaspoon | Salt, ⅛ teaspoon |
| Nut meats, 3 cups | Nut meats, 1½ cups |

Put the sugars, corn syrup, and water into a saucepan and cook, stirring until the sugar is dissolved. Continue cooking, stirring only enough to prevent scorching, until the temperature 300° F. is reached.

Remove from the fire, add salt, butter, and nut meats and stir only enough to mix well. If much stirring is done the brittle will sugar. It is desirable to have the nut meats warm before adding so that the candy will not harden before it can be put into the pans.

Set in a pan of hot water and with a large spoon dip out the candy and drop it into slightly buttered patty tins, making the candy layer only about one-fourth of an inch thick. When thoroughly cold, invert the tins and tap with a knife handle to loosen the patties. They should fall out of the tins.

These patties are very attractive when made in small tins —about one and one-half inches in diameter.

It is desirable to use unbroken nuts for patties. A mixture of different nuts may be used.

If these patties are to be kept they should be wrapped in waxed paper.

Cold water test when candy reaches 300° F.: very brittle.

Yield (large recipe): number of patties—twenty-four; weight—two and one-half pounds.

## COCOANUT BRITTLE

| LARGE RECIPE | SMALL RECIPE |
|---|---|
| Cocoanut, 1½ cups | Cocoanut, ¾ cup |
| Sugar, 2 cups | Sugar, 1 cup |
| Dark corn syrup, ½ cup | Dark corn syrup, ¼ cup |
| Water, ½ cup | Water, ¼ cup |
| Butter, 2 tablespoons | Butter, 1 tablespoon |
| Salt, ¼ teaspoon | Salt, ⅛ teaspoon |

Either fresh or desiccated cocoanut may be used in this recipe. If fresh cocoanut is used, prepare it according to directions given on page 97.

Brown the cocoanut in the oven at a low temperature for about ten minutes. If fresh cocoanut is used, a longer time will be required to allow for drying as well as for browning.

Put the sugar, corn syrup, and water into a saucepan and cook, stirring until the sugar is dissolved. Continue cooking, without stirring, until the temperature 265° F. is reached.

Add butter and salt and cook until candy reaches 300° F., stirring occasionally to prevent scorching.

Remove from fire and add cocoanut. Stir only enough to mix. If much stirring is done the brittle will sugar. Pour in a thin sheet on a greased slab or greased inverted pans or baking sheets. Do not scrape the saucepan, as this may cause the brittle to sugar. Have enough pans to give space for the brittle to be poured out in very thin sheets.

Flatten with a spatula, making the sheets as thin as possible.

While still warm, mark in squares.

Cold water test when candy reaches 265° F.: hard—almost brittle.

Cold water test when candy reaches 300° F.: amber color, crisp, very brittle.

Yield (large recipe): number of pieces—eighty (two inches square); weight—one and one-half pounds.

## CHOCOLATE BRITTLE

| LARGE RECIPE | SMALL RECIPE |
|---|---|
| Sugar, 2 cups | Sugar, 1 cup |
| Light corn syrup, ⅔ cup | Light corn syrup, ⅓ cup |
| Water, ½ cup | Water, ⅓ cup |
| Salt, ¼ teaspoon | Salt, ⅛ teaspoon |
| Chocolate, 2 squares (2 ounces) | Chocolate, 1 square (1 ounce) |
| Nut meats, 1 cup (broken in pieces) | Nut meats, ½ cup (broken in pieces) |
| Vanilla, 1 teaspoon | Vanilla, ½ teaspoon |

Melt the chocolate over hot water. Put the sugar, corn syrup, salt, and water into a saucepan and cook together, stirring until the sugar is dissolved. Continue cooking until the temperature 275° F. is reached.

Remove from the fire and add the melted chocolate, vanilla, and the broken nut meats. Stir only enough to mix the chocolate and nuts through the syrup.  If much stirring is done the brittle will sugar.  Pour on greased slab, inverted pans, or baking sheets.  Do not scrape the saucepan, as scraping may cause the brittle to sugar.  Have enough pans to give space for the brittle to be poured out in very thin sheets.

Smooth out with a spatula.  After about a half minute, take hold of the edges of the candy and, lifting it from the slab, pull it as thin as possible.

Break into irregular pieces.

English walnuts or pecans are very good in this brittle.

Cold water test when candy reaches 265° F.: hard, slightly brittle.

Yield (large recipe): number of pieces—thirty; weight—eighteen ounces.

## HONEY ALMOND CRISP

| LARGE RECIPE | SMALL RECIPE |
|---|---|
| Almonds, 1½ cups | Almonds, ¾ cup |
| Sugar, 2 cups | Sugar, 1 cup |
| Honey, ⅔ cup | Honey, ⅓ cup |
| Water, 1 cup | Water, ½ cup |
| Salt, ⅛ teaspoon | Salt, $\frac{1}{16}$ teaspoon |
| Butter, 2 tablespoons | Butter, 1 tablespoon |

Blanch the almonds, shred them, and heat them in a moderate oven until they are a delicate brown.

Put the sugar, honey, water, and salt into a saucepan and cook, stirring until the sugar is dissolved.  Continue cooking, without stirring, until the temperature 300°F. is reached.  If any sugar crystals form on the sides of the saucepan, they should be washed away with a piece of wet cloth.

Remove the candy from the fire.  Add butter and nut meats, and stir only enough to mix well.  If much stirring is done, the brittle will sugar.

Turn at once on a greased slab or a greased inverted pan or baking sheet.  Do not scrape the saucepan, as this may cause the brittle to sugar. Have enough pans to give space for the brittle to be poured out in very thin sheets.

Smooth out with a spatula. After about half a minute take hold of the edges of the candy and, lifting it slightly from the slab, pull as thin as possible. If the candy is in a large sheet, it may be necessary to cut off the thin pieces at the edges in order to pull the center.

Break into irregular pieces.

Cold water test when candy reaches 300° F.: very brittle.

Yield (large recipe): number of pieces—fifty; weight—one and one-quarter pounds.

## BUTTERSCOTCH

| LARGE RECIPE | SMALL RECIPE |
|---|---|
| Brown sugar, 2 cups | Brown sugar, 1 cup |
| Light corn syrup, ¼ cup | Light corn syrup, 2 table-spoons |
| Water, 1 cup | Water, ½ cup |
| Salt, ¼ teaspoon | Salt, ⅛ teaspoon |
| Butter, ⅓ cup | Butter, 3 tablespoons |
| Oil of lemon, 4 drops | Oil of lemon, 2 drops |

Put the sugar, corn syrup, salt, and water into a saucepan and cook, stirring until the sugar is dissolved. Continue cooking without stirring until the candy reaches the temperature 250° F.

Add butter and cook to 300° F., stirring to prevent scorching. Remove from fire, add oil of lemon, and pour in a thin sheet on a greased slab or a greased, inverted pan or baking sheet.

While still warm mark in small squares. The creases should be made quite deep so that the pieces can be easily separated. When cold break into pieces.

For a soft butterscotch cook to 270° F. after adding the butter. This will not be nearly so brittle as the one cooked to the higher temperature.

Cold water test when candy reaches 250° F.: hard ball.

Cold water test when candy reaches 300° F.: very brittle.

Yield (large recipe): number of pieces—one hundred (one inch square); weight—one and one-eighth pounds.

## ENGLISH TOFFEE

| LARGE RECIPE | SMALL RECIPE |
|---|---|
| Sugar, 2 cups | Sugar, 1 cup |
| Light corn syrup, 1½ cups | Light corn syrup, ¾ cup |
| Thin cream (or top milk), 1½ cups | Thin cream (or top milk), ¾ cup |
| Salt, ⅛ teaspoon | Salt, $\frac{1}{16}$ teaspoon |
| Butter, 3 tablespoons | Butter, 1½ tablespoons |
| Vanilla, 1 teaspoon | Vanilla, ½ teaspoon |

Put all of the ingredients except the butter and the vanilla into a saucepan and cook, stirring until the sugar is dissolved.

Continue cooking until the temperature 244° F. is reached. It will be necessary to stir this candy quite often, as it scorches easily. Add the butter and continue cooking to the temperature 252° F. Add vanilla.

Pour in a thin layer on a greased slab or an inverted pan or baking sheet which has been slightly greased. When still warm, mark with a knife in rectangular shapes about three inches long and one and one-fourth inches wide. The creases should be made quite deep so that the pieces of candy can be easily separated.

When cold the pieces can be broken apart along the lines of the creases.

This candy should be a little thicker than butterscotch. It should be slightly brittle—about as hard as the soft butterscotch.

Wrap each piece in waxed paper.

Cold water test when candy reaches 244° F.: rather firm ball.

Cold water test when candy reaches 252° F.: hard ball.

Yield (large recipe): number of pieces—one hundred (three by one and one-fourth inches); weight—one and one-fifth pounds.

**Nut Toffee.**—Use the recipe for English toffee and follow directions for cooking. When the toffee is done add one-half of a cup of almonds, blanched, cut into small pieces, and browned in the oven. Stir enough to mix through the candy. Pour in a thin layer on a greased slab or a greased inverted pan or baking sheet. While still warm mark in rectangular shapes—about three inches long by one and one-fourth inches wide. The creases should be made quite deep so that the pieces can be easily separated.

When cold, break the pieces apart and wrap in waxed paper.

Walnuts, hazel nuts, or pecans may be used if desired.

### BUTTER CRUNCH

> Sugar, 1 cup
> Butter, 1 cup
> Vanilla, ½ teaspoon
> Nuts, about 1 cup

Melt the butter over a low flame and add the sugar gradually, stirring until it is well blended with the butter, and with continued stirring cook it to 300° F. (brittle in cold water).

Add one-half cup of broken nut meats, if desired, and pour out on a smooth buttered surface. Spread thinly and cool for ten minutes. Coat with melted sweet chocolate and sprinkle with chopped nuts. When cold break into small pieces.

Yield: weight—one and one-fourth pounds.

**General Directions.**—In making hard candies, the essential thing is to avoid crystallization, so that the candy will be clear and bright. To avoid crystallization a large proportion of corn syrup to sugar is used. The candy is not stirred during the cooking, after the sugar has dissolved. The sides of the pan are washed with a wet cloth to remove any sugar crystals which may lodge there.

In addition to these precautions, stir only enough to mix the coloring and flavoring through the candy when these are added.

Darkening of the syrup can be avoided by cooking slowly during the last few minutes, and by selecting a pan of such a shape that the candy will not be spread out over too large a surface in cooking. The upper part of a one-quart double boiler is a good shape and size.

The flavoring should be added as soon as the candy is taken from the fire, and for this reason a good deal must be used because the high temperature of the syrup causes some of it to evaporate. The flavoring oils—not the extracts—should be used, because they are much stronger.

The following combinations of flavor and color are customary:

Oil of clove or cinnamon . . . . Red
Oil of lime or spearmint . . . . Green
Oil of wintergreen . . . . . . Pink
Oil of lemon . . . . . . . . Yellow

If a coloring paste is used, it should be completely dissolved in as little water as possible.

86

Hard candies readily become sticky in hot or moist weather. They should never be put in a box with unwrapped candy of another type, because they will absorb its moisture. They keep best if placed in a tightly covered tin box with waxed paper between the layers.

## LOLLYPOPS

| LARGE RECIPE | SMALL RECIPE |
|---|---|
| Sugar, 2 cups | Sugar, 1 cup |
| Light corn syrup, ⅔ cup | Light corn syrup, ⅓ cup |
| Water, 1 cup | Water, ⅔ cup |
| Oil of peppermint, ½ tea-spoon | Oil of peppermint, 8 drops |
| Coloring matter | Coloring matter |

Put the sugar, corn syrup, and water into a saucepan and cook, stirring until the sugar is dissolved. Continue cooking, without stirring, until the temperature 310° F. is reached. During the cooking wash the sides of the pan with a wet cloth to remove any sugar crystals. The last twenty degrees of cooking should be done more slowly, so that there will be no discoloration of the syrup along the sides of the saucepan.

When done, remove from the fire, add coloring and flavoring, and stir only enough to mix.

From this point work must be done very rapidly because the candy has been cooked to a high temperature and will harden quickly.

For small lollypops drop from the tip of a tablespoon on a smooth greased slab or a greased inverted platter or baking sheet. The surface must be level or the lollypops will not be round.

Press one end of a toothpick or skewer into the edge of each lollypop. If decorations are to be used on the lollypop, they should be placed on it while it is still warm, so that they can be pressed into the candy.

For larger lollypops, pour the syrup from the pan instead of dropping it from the spoon.

Loosen the lollypops from the slab as soon as they are firm, before they are entirely cold. If allowed to remain until hard they will crack when being taken up.

Lollypops can be made in fancy shapes by pouring the mixture in small, slightly greased molds. Such molds can be purchased in the form of rabbits, fish, lambs, dogs, etc. The sticks should be pressed in while the candy is still warm.

Cold water test when syrup reaches 310° F.: very brittle.

Yield (large recipe): number—twenty lollypops (about three inches in diameter).

**Decorated Lollypops.**—Decorated lollypops make original favors for parties, either for children or grown-ups. The decorations may be conventional designs, flowers, or faces. A great deal of originality can go into the scheme of decoration.

For the flowers or conventional designs, caraway comfits of assorted colors, candied cherries, shredded blanched almonds, ornamental frosting, or the tiny candies used in decorating cakes are suitable. Stems may be made of angelica and leaves of angelica or blanched pistachio nuts.

For the faces, the eyes may be made from currants. Eyes of white almond may have black currant pupils. For a wide-eyed baby, use white candy peppermint rings and put currants in the holes in the centers. Strips of shredded raisins can be used for shaggy eye-brows. Beetling brows from black jelly beans give expression to a face.

A jelly bean nose isn't exactly Roman, but it will do. Or you can use strips of almond or candied fruit.

Almost anything will do for a mouth. If the lollypop is of another color than red, candied cherries give the effect of red lips. Strips of candied apricot or black prunes can be shaped to form mouths with turned up or turned down corners.

The effect of bangs can be achieved by sprinkling small

candies or chopped nuts in the place where the hair ought to be.

For success in decorating lollypops, the design must be selected and the materials for carrying it out must be at hand before the lollypops are dropped. The lollypops harden quickly, and unless the design is pressed in at once the pieces will fall off.

If two persons work together, one can drop the lollypops and put in the skewer handles, while the other does the decorating. If one person works alone, she should drop a few lollypops and then set the saucepan of syrup in hot water so that it will not harden while she does the decorating.

**Spiced Hard Candies.**—Use the recipe for lollypops, substituting oil of clove or cinnamon for the peppermint, and coloring the syrup red.

For squares, pour in a thin sheet on a slightly greased slab or a greased inverted platter, pan, or baking sheet. Mark deeply while still warm. When cool loosen the sheet of candy, lift from the slab, and break into squares. It is very difficult to make perfect squares. For the amateur candy maker it is probably better to make patties or small molds.

For patties, pour thin layers of the mixture into slightly greased muffin pans of the smallest size. When firm, invert the pan over a clean tea towel and loosen the candies by tapping on the bottom of the pan. The towel is used to prevent the candy from falling on a hard surface and breaking. Do not allow the candy to stand too long in the molds or the patties will be so brittle they will break while being removed.

The patties may be decorated while they are still warm and soft in the pans. A simple but effective decoration is obtained by sprinkling the patties with candies of mixed colors.

Tiny, round candy moons can be made by dropping small amounts of syrup from the tip of a teaspoon. These also can be decorated. If bright contrasting colors with suitable flavors are used, they will add much to the attractiveness of a candy box.

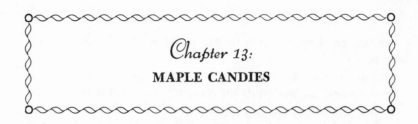

**General Directions.**—In sections of the country where maple sugar and syrup are plentiful, the candies made from them are cheap. Even where they are more expensive, we like to use them occasionally both on account of their delicious flavor and because they are not quite so sweet as cane sugar.

When either maple sugar or syrup is used in a recipe containing milk, the candy should be stirred continually while cooking as the acid in the maple may cause the milk to curdle.

When maple sugar is used it should be broken into small pieces and the candy cooked slowly at first, until the sugar is completely dissolved. If the sugar is old and very hard, it may be necessary to use extra water.

## MAPLE TAFFY

| LARGE RECIPE | SMALL RECIPE |
|---|---|
| Sugar, ½ cup | Sugar, ⅓ cup |
| Light corn syrup, ¾ cup | Light corn syrup, ½ cup |
| Maple syrup, ¾ cup | Maple syrup, ½ cup |
| Water, ⅓ cup | Water, ¼ cup |
| Soda, ⅛ teaspoon | Soda, $\frac{1}{16}$ teaspoon |
| Butter, 1½ tablespoons | Butter, 1 tablespoon |

Put the sugar, corn syrup, maple syrup, and water into a saucepan, and cook, stirring until the sugar is dissolved. Continue cooking, stirring occasionally to prevent burning, until the temperature 275° F. is reached.

When the candy is cooked to 275° F., it is quite hard. If a softer taffy is desired, cook only to 270° F.

Remove from the fire, add the butter and soda (free from lumps), and stir just enough to mix well. Too much stirring may cause the taffy to sugar.

Turn into a greased pan and allow to stand until it is cool enough to handle.

Gather into a ball and pull until light in color and rather firm. Stretch out in a long rope and cut into pieces with the scissors. If not to be used at once, wrap in waxed paper.

Cold water test when the candy reaches 275° F.: slightly brittle.

Yield (large recipe): number of pieces—seventy-five; weight —fifteen ounces.

## MAPLE SUGAR PATTIES

| LARGE RECIPE | SMALL RECIPE |
|---|---|
| Maple sugar, 2¼ cups (1 pound) | Maple sugar, 1⅛ cups (½ pound) |
| Water, 2 cups | Water, 1 cup |

Cook together in a saucepan, stirring only until the sugar is dissolved. Continue cooking until the temperature 238° F. is reached. Remove from the fire.

For patties of quite a smooth texture, cool the syrup to 110° F. (lukewarm) before beating. Then beat until it begins to look creamy and loses its gloss. Turn into greased patty tins. These patties will be quite light in color.

For patties of a darker color and more grainy texture begin to beat candy as soon as it is taken from the fire. Continue beating until thick and slightly sugary on the edge of the pan. Turn into patty tins which have been greased. Set aside for a day to harden.

Cold water test when the candy reaches 238° F.: soft ball.

Yield (large recipe): number of patties—twenty; weight— one pound.

## MAPLE SUGAR FONDANT

| LARGE RECIPE | SMALL RECIPE |
|---|---|
| Maple sugar, 2¼ cups (1 pound) | Maple sugar, 1⅛ cups (½ pound) |
| Light corn syrup, 2 tablespoons | Light corn syrup, 1 tablespoon |
| Water, 1 cup | Water, ¾ cup |
| Vanilla, 1 teaspoon | Vanilla, ½ teaspoon |

Break the maple sugar into pieces and put it into a saucepan with the water and corn syrup. Cook, stirring constantly, until the sugar is dissolved. Remove the spoon and do not stir again during the cooking.

When the candy begins to boil, cover the saucepan and cook for three minutes. The steam formed washes down any sugar crystals which may be thrown on the sides of the saucepan. Remove the cover and continue the cooking.

From time to time wash down any sugar crystals which appear on the sides of the saucepan. For this purpose a fork covered with cheesecloth and dipped into cold water may be used.

Cook to 238° F.

Remove from fire and pour at once on a cold, wet platter. Cool to 110° F. (lukewarm). Beat with a fondant paddle or a spatula until the fondant becomes light and creamy. Add vanilla and knead until the mass is creamy and no lumps remain. A long beating is required for maple fondant.

Put away in a crock or glass jar and allow to ripen for two or three days before using. The fondant can be kept three or four weeks if waxed paper is laid over it and if it is kept tightly covered. If it becomes too dry, it should be covered with a damp cloth.

Cold water test when fondant is cooked to 238° F.: soft ball.

Yield (large recipe): weight—one pound.

## MAPLE BROWN SUGAR FONDANT

LARGE RECIPE
Brown sugar, 2 cups
Maple syrup, 1 cup
Water, 1 cup

SMALL RECIPE
Brown sugar, 1 cup
Maple syrup, ½ cup
Water, ½ cup

Put the sugar, syrup, and water into a saucepan and cook, stirring, until the sugar is dissolved. Continue the cooking, without stirring, until the temperature 240° F. is reached. If sugar crystals form on the sides of the pan, they should be washed away with a wet cloth.

Remove from fire, pour on a cold wet platter; cool to 110° F. (lukewarm). Beat until creamy. A long beating is required. When the fondant can be handled, knead it until creamy and free from lumps.

This fondant is delicious for centers for chocolates.

(For more detailed directions for cooking, see maple sugar fondant, page 92.)

Cold water test when candy reaches 240° F.: rather firm ball.

Yield (large recipe): weight—one pound.

## MAPLE CREAMS

LARGE RECIPE
Maple sugar, 1⅛ cups
  (½ pound)
Granulated sugar, 1 cup
Water, ⅓ cup
Milk, ¾ cup
Corn syrup, 2 tablespoons
Butter, 1 tablespoon
Vanilla, 1 teaspoon

SMALL RECIPE
Maple sugar, ⅝ cup
  (¼ pound)
Granulated sugar, ½ cup
Water, ¼ cup
Milk, ½ cup
Corn syrup, 1 tablespoon
Butter, ½ tablespoon
Vanilla, ½ teaspoon

Break the maple sugar into pieces.

Cook the water and maple sugar together, stirring until the sugar dissolves.

Add the milk, corn syrup, and granulated sugar and cook, stirring, until the temperature 236° F. is reached. Remove from the fire and add butter without stirring.

Cool to 110° F. (lukewarm), add vanilla, and beat until the candy becomes creamy. Turn into slightly greased pans. When cool, cut into squares.

This candy is very delicate in flavor. The maple flavor is less pronounced than in the maple nut squares.

Black walnuts, or other nuts, may be added if desired.

Cold water test when candy reaches 236° F.: soft ball.

Yield (large recipe): number of pieces—twenty-four; weight—one pound.

## MAPLE NUT SQUARES

| LARGE RECIPE | SMALL RECIPE |
|---|---|
| Maple sugar, 2¼ cups (1 pound) | Maple sugar, 1⅛ cups (½ pound) |
| Water, ¾ cup | Water, ½ cup |
| Light corn syrup, 1 tablespoon | Light corn syrup, ½ tablespoon |
| Thin cream, ¾ cup | Thin cream, ⅜ cup |
| Nut meats, ⅔ cup (broken in pieces) | Nut meats, ⅓ cup (broken in pieces) |

Break the maple sugar into pieces and put it with the water and syrup into a saucepan. Cook, stirring until the sugar is dissolved. Add the cream and cook, stirring, to prevent curdling, until the temperature 238° F. is reached.

Remove from the fire. Cool to 110° F. (lukewarm). Beat until the candy becomes creamy and until a small amount of it, dropped from the spoon, will hold its shape. Add nuts and turn the candy into slightly greased pans. Pecans or walnuts are especially good with the maple flavor.

This candy requires a long beating and is very creamy.

When cold cut into squares the size of caramels.

Cold water test when candy reaches 238° F.: soft ball.

Yield (large recipe): number of pieces—thirty-six; weight—one and one-fourth pounds.

## MAPLE NUT BRITTLE

| LARGE RECIPE | SMALL RECIPE |
|---|---|
| Maple sugar, 1 cup (⅖ pound) | Maple sugar, ½ cup (⅕ pound) |
| Light corn syrup, 1 cup | Light corn syrup, ½ cup |
| Water, ½ cup | Water, ⅓ cup |
| Nut meats, 1 cup | Nut meats, ½ cup |
| Butter, 2 tablespoons | Butter, 1 tablespoon |

Break the nut meats into pieces and heat them in a moderate oven until crisp and slightly brown. Pecans, walnuts, hickory nuts, or almonds blend especially well with the maple flavor.

Put the sugar, syrup, and water into a saucepan and cook, stirring until the sugar is dissolved. If the sugar is old and hard, use a low flame during the first part of the cooking. Continue cooking, without stirring, until the temperature 275° F. is reached. If sugar crystals form on the sides of the pan during the cooking, they should be washed away with a piece of wet cloth.

Add butter and nut meats, and cook, stirring to prevent burning, until the temperature 290° F. is reached. Remove from the fire. Turn at once on a greased slab or a greased, inverted pan or baking sheet. Do not scrape the saucepan, as this may cause the brittle to sugar. Have enough pans to give space for the brittle to be poured out in very thin sheets.

Smooth with a spatula. After about half a minute, take hold of the edges of the candy, and, lifting it slightly from the slab, pull as thin as possible. If the candy is in a large sheet, it may be necessary to break off the thin pieces at the edges in order to pull the center.

Break into irregular pieces.

Cold water test when candy reaches 275° F.: slightly brittle.

Cold water test when candy reaches 290° F.: very brittle.

Yield (large recipe): number of pieces—thirty; weight—thirteen ounces.

## MAPLE PENUCHI

| LARGE RECIPE | SMALL RECIPE |
|---|---|
| Brown sugar, ½ cup | Brown sugar, ¼ cup |
| Granulated sugar, 1½ cups | Granulated sugar, ¾ cup |
| Maple syrup, 1 cup | Maple syrup, ½ cup |
| Milk, ½ cup | Milk, ¼ cup |
| Light corn syrup, 2 tablespoons | Light corn syrup, 1 tablespoon |
| Butter, 1 tablespoon | Butter, ½ tablespoon |
| Nut meats, 1 cup (pecans or walnuts) | Nut meats, ½ cup (pecans or walnuts) |
| Vanilla, 1 teaspoon | Vanilla, ½ teaspoon |

Put the sugars, syrups, and milk into a saucepan. Cook, stirring constantly, to a temperature of 236° F.

Remove from the fire, add butter, and set aside to cool. When lukewarm (110° F.) add vanilla and broken nuts, and beat until thick and creamy. Pour into slightly greased pans. When cold, cut into squares.

Cold water test when candy reaches 236° F.: soft ball.

Yield (large recipe): number of pieces—twenty-four; weight—one and three-fourths pounds.

# Chapter 14:

## COCOANUT CANDIES

**General Directions.**—There are three kinds of cocoanut usually available for candy making: the dry or desiccated, the fresh, and the canned fresh. The fresh cocoanut and the canned fresh cocoanut are both much more moist than the dried, hence it is not safe to substitute one for the other in the recipes given. The canned fresh cocoanut may be substituted for the fresh grated by draining the canned cocoanut in a cheesecloth or fine sieve and putting in an equal measure. To open the fresh cocoanut, remove the eye with a sharp pointed knife and drain out the cocoanut milk through this opening. Break the cocoanut with a hatchet, small axe, or chisel. Remove the cocoanut meat. Cut off the brown rind. The cocoanut may then be grated or sliced in very thin slices with a sharp knife.

One cocoanut yields about three-fourths of a cup of milk. If any recipe calls for this amount of milk and the cocoanut does not yield enough, add water to make up the required liquid measurement.

One cocoanut yields about four cups of grated cocoanut. This should be measured lightly—not packed.

### FRESH COCOANUT DROPS

| LARGE RECIPE | SMALL RECIPE |
|---|---|
| Fondant, 2 cups | Fondant, 1 cup |
| Fresh cocoanut, grated, 1 cup | Fresh cocoanut, grated, ½ cup |
| Vanilla, 1 teaspoon | Vanilla, ½ teaspoon |

Knead together the fondant and cocoanut. Put into the upper part of the double boiler, over hot water, and heat until melted.   Do not allow the water to boil while melting the fondant.

When soft add vanilla and drop from the tip of a teaspoon on a slightly greased slab or inverted pan.

When dropped, the fondant mixture should be firm enough to hold its shape in small mounds.   These should not be more than an inch in diameter.

For more detailed directions for melting fondant, see Chapter V, page 28.

Yield (large recipe): number of pieces—seventy small drops.

## COCOANUT LADY CREAMS

| LARGE RECIPE | SMALL RECIPE |
|---|---|
| Sugar, 2 cups | Sugar, 1 cup |
| Cocoanut milk, ¾ cup | Cocoanut milk, ⅜ cup |
| Water, ¼ cup | Water, ¼ cup |
| Fresh cocoanut, grated, 1 cup | Fresh cocoanut, grated, ½ cup |

Cook together the cocoanut milk, water, and sugar, stirring only until the sugar is dissolved.   Continue cooking, without stirring, until the temperature 240° F. is reached.   Wash down crystals which form on the sides of the pan.   (See general directions for fondant making, page 21.)

When the candy reaches 240° F. remove from the fire and pour on a wet platter.   Cool, without jarring, to the temperature 110° F. (lukewarm).

Beat with a fondant paddle, or spatula, until it becomes thick and creamy.   Knead for about four minutes, until it is smooth.

Add the fresh grated cocoanut, kneading it through the candy.   This softens the candy, making it almost too soft to handle.

Place the candy in the upper part of a double boiler and melt over hot water, stirring as little as possible.   If the candy is very soft allow it to stand over the hot water for about five minutes.

This candy may then be dropped from the tip of a teaspoon on a greased slab or inverted pan. Or it may be poured into small patty tins which have been dusted with cornstarch.

For the real lady-creams the candy should be poured into pans and allowed to stand until firm. Cut into bars about two by five inches and cover with coating-chocolate.

Cold water test when candy reaches 240° F.: soft ball.

Yield (large recipe): number of pieces—sixty or three bars; weight—fourteen ounces.

## ORANGE COCOANUT PATTIES

| LARGE RECIPE | SMALL RECIPE |
|---|---|
| Sugar, 2 cups | Sugar, 1 cup |
| Light corn syrup, 2 table-spoons | Light corn syrup, 1 table-spoon |
| Water, ¾ cup | Water, ½ cup |
| Fresh cocoanut, grated, ½ cup | Fresh cocoanut, grated, ¼ cup |
| Orange rind, grated, ½ teaspoon | Orange rind, grated, ¼ teaspoon |

Cook together the sugar, water, and corn syrup, stirring only until the sugar is dissolved. Continue cooking, without stirring, until the temperature 246° F. is reached. If sugar crystals form on the sides of the pan they should be washed away with a wet cloth. Remove from fire.

Add grated cocoanut and orange rind, taking care to stir as little as possible lest the mixture "sugar."

Pour out on a moist platter. Cool to 120° F. and then beat with a fondant paddle or a spatula. When it becomes thick and creamy knead for about four minutes—until it is smooth.

Color a delicate yellow or orange.

This fondant may be remelted and dropped on waxed paper.

It may be made into a bar and coated with chocolate. Or it may be shaped and rolled in cocoanut.

Measure the orange rind carefully, as an excess will completely mask the delicate taste of the fresh cocoanut.

Cold water test when the candy reaches 246° F.: firm ball.

Yield (large recipe): weight—one pound.

## FRESH COCOANUT CREAMS

| LARGE RECIPE | SMALL RECIPE |
|---|---|
| Fresh cocoanut, grated and browned, ¾ cup | Fresh cocoanut, grated and browned, ⅜ cup |
| Sugar, 2 cups | Sugar, 1 cup |
| Milk, ¾ cup | Milk, ⅜ cup |
| Light corn syrup, 1 tablespoon | Light corn syrup, ½ tablespoon |
| Butter, 1 tablespoon | Butter, ½ tablespoon |
| Vanilla, 1 teaspoon | Vanilla, ½ teaspoon |

The cocoanut may be browned or used without browning, as desired. If not browned it should be spread in a thin sheet and dried slightly to prevent excessive softening of the creams.

To brown: spread out in a very thin sheet on a pan and heat in a very slow oven (280° F.) for about twenty minutes.

Put the sugar, milk, and corn syrup into a saucepan and cook, stirring until the sugar is dissolved.

Continue cooking, stirring occasionally to prevent burning, until the temperature 240° F. is reached. Remove from the fire, add the butter. Stir only enough to mix the butter through the mass.

Pour on a platter which has been rinsed with cold water. Allow the candy to cool to 110° F., add vanilla, and beat with a fondant paddle until the mass becomes creamy. Knead, working in the cocoanut.

Press into slightly buttered pans and when cold cut into squares about the size of caramels.

Cold water test when candy reaches 240° F.: soft ball.

Yield (large recipe): number of pieces—twenty-four squares; weight—one and one-eighth pounds.

## COCOANUT SNOWBALLS

| LARGE RECIPE | SMALL RECIPE |
|---|---|
| Sugar, 2½ cups | Sugar, 1¼ cups |
| Light corn syrup, 2 table-spoons | Light corn syrup, 1 table-spoon |
| Water, ¾ cup | Water, ½ cup |
| Fresh cocoanut, grated, 2 cups | Fresh cocoanut, grated, 1 cup |

Cook all of the ingredients together until the temperature 238° F. is reached. Stir until the sugar is dissolved when beginning the cooking, and thereafter stir as little as possible to prevent burning.

If sugar crystals appear on the sides of the saucepan during cooking, wash them down with a damp cloth as in making fondant.

When the candy is done, remove from the fire at once and pour into a dampened platter. Do not scrape the kettle, as it may cause the candy to "sugar."

Cool the candy to 120° F. and beat it with a fondant paddle or a spatula. When thick and creamy knead it until smooth and free from lumps.

Shape in small balls. These may be rolled in grated cocoanut or in granulated sugar to give them a more irregular appearance.

Cold water test when the candy reaches 238° F.: soft ball.

Yield (large recipe): number of pieces—fifty snowballs; weight—one and one-half pounds.

## COCOANUT SANDUSKYS

| LARGE RECIPE | SMALL RECIPE |
|---|---|
| Granulated sugar, 1 cup | Granulated sugar, ½ cup |
| Brown sugar, 1 cup | Brown sugar, ½ cup |
| Cocoanut milk, ½ cup | Cocoanut milk, ¼ cup |
| Water, ¼ cup | Water, ¼ cup |
| Fresh cocoanut, grated, 1 cup | Fresh cocoanut, grated, ½ cup |
| Vanilla, 1 teaspoon | Vanilla, ½ teaspoon |

Water may be substituted for the cocoanut milk if desired.

Cook together the cocoanut, cocoanut milk, sugar, and water until the temperature 236° F. is reached. Stir during cooking to prevent burning.

Remove from fire and cool to 120° F. Beat until thick and creamy. This requires a long beating.

Turn into greased pans. Cut in squares.

This is a rather soft candy. If you wish a firmer candy, which can be cut and served soon after making, cook to 238° F.

Cold water test when the candy reaches 236° F.: soft ball.

Yield (large recipe): number of pieces—twevle; weight—thirteen ounces.

## COCOANUT SNOWFLAKES

| LARGE RECIPE | SMALL RECIPE |
|---|---|
| Sugar, 2 cups | Sugar, 1 cup |
| Light corn syrup, 2 tablespoons | Light corn syrup, 1 tablespoon |
| Water, ¾ cup | Water, ½ cup |
| Fondant, melted, ⅔ cup | Fondant, melted, ⅓ cup |
| Fresh cocoanut, grated, 2 cups | Fresh cocoanut, grated, 1 cup |
| Vanilla, 1 teaspoon | Vanilla, ½ teaspoon |

Put the sugar and water into a saucepan and cook, stirring until the sugar is dissolved. Continue the cooking, stirring only enough to prevent burning, until the temperature 270° F. is reached.  If sugar crystals form on the sides of the pan, they should be washed away with a damp cloth.

Remove the candy from the fire, add the fondant, which has been melted over hot water, and the cocoanut.  Mix thoroughly.  Add vanilla.  Pour on a greased slab or inverted baking sheet.  When firm cut into squares or bars.  Because of the large amount of cocoanut, the candy is somewhat rough in appearance.  It should be cut while warm.

The candy may be dropped by the teaspoonful on a greased surface and shaped with the spoon to resemble snowballs.

Cold water test when candy reaches 270° F.: almost brittle.

Yield (large recipe): number of bars—twenty-four (one inch wide and three inches long); weight—one and three-fourths pounds.

## FRESH COCOANUT CRISP

| LARGE RECIPE | SMALL RECIPE |
|---|---|
| Light corn syrup, ¾ cup | Light corn syrup, ⅓ cup |
| Sugar, 1¼ cups | Sugar, ¾ cup |
| Fresh cocoanut, sliced, 1½ cups | Fresh cocoanut, sliced, ¾ cup |

Put the sugar and syrup into a saucepan and cook slowly, stirring until the sugar is dissolved.  Continue cooking, stirring occasionally, until the temperature 250° F. is reached.

Add the cocoanut and cook slowly, stirring constantly, until the cocoanut becomes brown.  The temperature will then be about 275° F.

Pour the candy on a greased slab or greased inverted baking sheet.  Spread it out in a thin sheet.  After about a half minute take hold of the edges of the candy, and lifting it slightly from the slab, pull it as thin as possible.  If the candy is in a large sheet it may be necessary to break off the thin pieces at the edges in order to pull the center.

Break into irregular pieces.

Cold water test when candy reaches 250° F.: very firm, beginning to get brittle.

Cold water test when candy reaches 275° F.: brittle.

Yield (large recipe): weight—one pound.

## FRESH COCOANUT BRITTLE

| LARGE RECIPE | SMALL RECIPE |
|---|---|
| Granulated sugar, 2 cups | Granulated sugar, 1 cup |
| Brown sugar, 1 cup | Brown sugar, ½ cup |
| Light corn syrup, ½ cup | Light corn syrup, ¼ cup |
| Water, ½ cup | Water, ¼ cup |
| Butter, 2 tablespoons | Butter, 1 tablespoon |
| Soda, ⅛ teaspoon | Soda, $\frac{1}{16}$ teaspoon |
| Salt, ⅛ teaspoon | Salt, $\frac{1}{16}$ teaspoon |
| Fresh cocoanut, sliced, 1½ cups | Fresh cocoanut, sliced, ¾ cup |

Brown the sliced, fresh cocoanut in the oven.

Put the sugar, water, and corn syrup into a saucepan and cook, stirring until the sugar is dissolved.  Continue cooking, without stirring, until the candy reaches 300° F.  Wash down sugar crystals from the sides of the pan with a damp cloth.

Remove from fire, add salt, soda (free from lumps), and butter, and stir only enough to mix well.  Add the browned cocoanut, stir, and turn at once on a greased slab or inverted pan or baking sheet.

Smooth out with a spatula.  After about a minute take hold of the edges of the candy, and lifting it slightly from the slab, pull it as thin as possible.

Break into irregular pieces.

Cold water test when candy reaches 300° F.: very brittle.

Yield (large recipe): weight—one and three-fourths pounds.

## COCOANUT HAYSTACKS

| LARGE RECIPE | SMALL RECIPE |
|---|---|
| Granulated sugar, 1 cup | Granulated sugar, ½ cup |
| Brown sugar, 1 cup | Brown sugar, ½ cup |
| Water, ¾ cup | Water, ⅜ cup |
| Dark corn syrup, 1 cup | Dark corn syrup, ½ cup |
| Butter, 2 tablespoons | Butter, 1 tablespoon |
| Salt, ½ teaspoon | Salt, ¼ teaspoon |
| Desiccated cocoanut, 4½ cups | Desiccated cocoanut, 2¼ cups |

If the cocoanut is very coarse it should be chopped.

The flavor is improved if the cocoanut is heated in the oven until a delicate brown.

Put all the ingredients except the cocoanut into a saucepan and cook, stirring until the sugar is dissolved. Continue cooking, stirring only enough to prevent burning, until the temperature 245° F. is reached.

Remove from the fire, add cocoanut. Mix thoroughly. Drop by spoonfuls on a greased surface and shape into cones with the hands. Work quickly or the mixture will harden.

Cold water test when candy reaches 245° F.: firm ball, but not hard (about like a soft caramel).

Yield (large recipe): number of haystacks—twenty-eight; weight—one and one-fourth pounds.

## COCOANUT CUBES

| LARGE RECIPE | SMALL RECIPE |
|---|---|
| Sugar, 1½ cups | Sugar, ¾ cup |
| Light corn syrup, 2 cups | Light corn syrup, 1 cup |
| Water, ¼ cup | Water, ¼ cup |
| Fondant, 2 cups | Fondant, 1 cup |
| Desiccated cocoanut, 2 cups | Desiccated cocoanut, 1 cup |

Heat the cocoanut in a moderate oven until a delicate brown.

Cook together the sugar, corn syrup, and water, stirring

until the sugar is dissolved.  Continue cooking, without stirring, until the temperature 254° F. is reached.

Remove from the fire, add the fondant and cocoanut, stir until thoroughly mixed, and pour into greased pans.  When still lukewarm, cut into cubes of desired size.

These may be wrapped, as caramels, or served unwrapped.

Coffee, caramel, and brown sugar fondant are better in this recipe than a plain vanilla fondant because their flavor is more pronounced.  The darker colors also improve the appearance of this candy.

Cold water test when candy reaches 254° F.: hard ball.

Yield (large recipe): number of pieces—ninety-six (size of caramels); weight—three pounds.

# Chapter 15:

## POP CORN CANDIES

**General Directions for Popping Corn.**—Corn can be popped either in a regular popper or in an iron frying pan. When using the popper, do not put in too much unpopped corn at one time, because the popper will become so full that the last of the batch will not have room to pop. It is better to pop over a covered or a low flame so that the pop corn will not be scorched. Shake the popper constantly during the process.

Many persons prefer to use an iron frying pan, believing that the popped corn has a better flavor and is less dry. Melt one tablespoon of lard or any vegetable shortening and one of butter in a large frying pan. To this add one-half cup of pop corn, cover, and shake the frying pan over the fire until the corn is popped. Bacon fat can be substituted if the flavor is desired.

If the corn does not pop well it can be covered with water for about three minutes, drained, and dried on clean tea towels. This additional moisture often causes the corn to pop.

After corn is popped it can be salted, or salted and buttered. Melt the butter and pour it over the corn, stirring the corn as you pour. The amount of butter to be used depends upon personal taste.

One cup of corn will yield about five cups.

**Pop Corn Balls.**—Use only the large, well-popped kernels for balls. Sort out and reject the hard pieces of corn which have not completely popped. Some of these can be chopped and used for cornlets or crisp.

A small amount of salt put on the popped corn will add to the flavor of the balls, but less should be used than when the popped corn is to be served buttered.

Put the popped corn into a large bowl so that there will be plenty of room to stir the corn while the syrup is being added. After the syrup has been poured over the corn, it will be necessary to shape the balls quickly. When working with large quantities, pour the hot syrup over only a portion of the popped corn at a time and form balls from this. Set the pan containing the remainder of the syrup in a pan of hot water until ready to use. In this way the syrup will not have a chance to cool and harden before the balls can be shaped.

In forming pop corn balls use as little pressure as possible so that the kernels will not be crushed and so that the balls will be less compact.

Any dry, ready to eat cereal may be satisfactorily substituted for popped corn.

## MOLASSES POP CORN BALLS

| LARGE RECIPE | SMALL RECIPE |
|---|---|
| Light molasses, 1 cup | Light molasses, ½ cup |
| Dark corn syrup, 1 cup | Dark corn syrup, ½ cup |
| Vinegar, 1 tablespoon | Vinegar, ½ tablespoon |
| Butter, 3 tablespoons | Butter, 1½ tablespoons |
| Popped corn, 3 quarts | Popped corn, 1½ quarts |
| Salt, ½ teaspoon | Salt, ¼ teaspoon |

Mix molasses, syrup, and vinegar in a saucepan and cook, stirring occasionally to prevent burning, until the temperature 270° F. is reached. After 240° F. is reached, constant stirring will be necessary. When done add butter and stir only enough to mix. Slowly pour the cooked syrup over the salted popped corn and mix well.

Form into balls with the hands, using as little pressure as possible.

Two drops of oil of lemon may be added to the syrup.

Cold water test when syrup reaches 270° F.: slightly brittle.

Yield (large recipe): number of balls—twenty (two and one-half inches in diameter).

## HONEY POP CORN BALLS

LARGE RECIPE
Strained honey, ¾ cup
Light corn syrup, 1¼ cups
Butter, 1 tablespoon
Vinegar, ½ tablespoon
Popped corn, 3 quarts
Salt, 1 teaspoon

SMALL RECIPE
Strained honey, ½ cup
Light corn syrup, ½ cup
Butter, ½ tablespoon
Vinegar, 1 teaspoon
Popped corn, 1½ quarts
Salt, ½ teaspoon

Cook together in a saucepan the honey, syrup, and vinegar until the temperature 275° F. is reached, stirring occasionally to prevent burning. During the latter part of the cooking almost constant stirring will be necessary. When done, add butter and stir only enough to mix.

Pour the cooked syrup slowly over the salted popped corn and mix well. Form into balls with the hands.

Cold water test when candy reaches 275° F.: slightly brittle.

Yield (large recipe): number of balls—fifteen (three inches in diameter).

## SOFT POP CORN BALLS

LARGE RECIPE
Granulated sugar, 1 cup
Brown sugar, 1 cup
Light corn syrup, ⅓ cup
Water, ½ cup
Butter, 1 tablespoon
Popped corn, 3 quarts
Salt, 1 teaspoon

SMALL RECIPE
Granulated sugar, ½ cup
Brown sugar, ½ cup
Light corn syrup, 2 table-
spoons
Water, ⅓ cup
Butter, ½ tablespoon
Popped corn, 1½ quarts
Salt, ½ teaspoon

Put the granulated sugar, brown sugar, syrup, and water into a saucepan and cook, stirring until the sugar is dissolved. Continue cooking, without stirring, until the temperature 240° F. is reached. Add the butter and stir only enough to mix it through the candy.

Have the popped corn in a large bowl so that when the syrup is added there will be room enough for thorough mixing. Pour the cooked syrup slowly over the salted popped corn. Mix well. Form into balls with the hands, using as little pressure as possible.

These balls are rather soft. If firmer balls are desired, cook the syrup to 242° F.

Cold water test when syrup reaches 240° F.: soft ball.

Yield (large recipe): number of balls—twenty (two and one-half inches in diameter).

## PINK POP CORN BALLS

| LARGE RECIPE | SMALL RECIPE |
| --- | --- |
| Sugar, 2 cups | Sugar, 1 cup |
| Light corn syrup, 2 tablespoons | Light corn syrup, 1 tablespoon |
| Water, 1¼ cups | Water, ¾ cup |
| Pink coloring, few drops | Pink coloring, few drops |
| Vanilla, 1 teaspoon | Vanilla, ½ teaspoon |
| Popped corn, 3 quarts | Popped corn, 1½ quarts |
| Salt, 1 teaspoon | Salt, ½ teaspoon |

Put the sugar, corn syrup, and water into a saucepan and cook, stirring until the sugar is dissolved. Continue cooking, without stirring, until the temperature 290° F. is reached (brittle in cold water). Add the vanilla and the coloring paste which has been dissolved in as little water as possible. Stir only enough to mix the coloring evenly.

Have the popped corn in a large bowl and sprinkle with the salt. Pour the cooked syrup slowly over the salted popped corn, stirring well.

Form into balls with the hands, using little pressure.

Cold water test when syrup reaches 290° F.: brittle.

Yield (large recipe): number of balls—twenty (two and one-half inches in diameter).

## MAPLE POP CORN BALLS

| LARGE RECIPE | SMALL RECIPE |
|---|---|
| Maple sugar, ½ cup | Maple sugar, ¼ cup |
| Light corn syrup, 1 cup | Light corn syrup, ½ cup |
| Butter, 1 tablespoon | Butter, ½ tablespoon |
| Popped corn, 2½ quarts | Popped corn, 5 cups |
| Salt, 1 teaspoon | Salt, ½ teaspoon |

Cook together the maple sugar and corn syrup, stirring constantly until the sugar is dissolved. Continue cooking, stirring occasionally, until the temperature 275° F. is reached. Remove from fire, add butter, and stir only enough to mix. Pour the cooked syrup slowly over the salted popped corn; mix well.

Form into balls with the hands, using as little pressure as possible.

Cold water test when syrup reaches 275° F.: hard, almost brittle.

Yield (large recipe): number of balls—ten (two inches in diameter).

## POP CORN BRICKS

| LARGE RECIPE | SMALL RECIPE |
|---|---|
| Popped corn, 5 cups | Popped corn, 2½ cups |
| Peanuts, shelled, 2 cups | Peanuts, shelled, 1 cup |
| Molasses, ½ cup | Molasses, ¼ cup |
| Brown sugar, 1 cup | Brown sugar, ½ cup |
| Vinegar, ½ tablespoon | Vinegar, 1 teaspoon |
| Butter, ½ tablespoon | Butter, 1 teaspoon |
| Salt, ½ teaspoon | Salt, ¼ teaspoon |

Select large, well-popped grains of corn. Brown the peanuts in the oven.

Cook together the molasses, sugar, and vinegar, stirring enough to prevent burning. Boil until the temperature 275° F. is reached. Add butter and peanuts to syrup and stir only enough to mix. Pour the hot syrup and peanuts over the salted popped corn, stirring during the addition. Mold into bricks by pressing the mixture into greased pans, four by six inches in size. Use as little pressure as possible so as to prevent breaking the corn.

Cold water test when candy reaches 275° F.: hard, almost brittle.

Yield (large recipe): number of bricks—eight.

## POP CORN CRISP

| LARGE RECIPE | SMALL RECIPE |
|---|---|
| Granulated sugar, 1½ cups | Granulated sugar, ¾ cup |
| Brown sugar, 1½ cups | Brown sugar, ¾ cup |
| Dark corn syrup, ½ cup | Dark corn syrup, ¼ cup |
| Water, ½ cup | Water, ¼ cup |
| Butter, 2 tablespoons | Butter, 1 tablespoon |
| Salt, ½ teaspoon | Salt, ¼ teaspoon |
| Popped corn, chopped, 1½ cups | Popped corn, chopped, ¾ cup |

Put the sugars, water, and corn syrup into a saucepan and cook, stirring until the sugars are dissolved. Continue cooking, without stirring, until the candy reaches the temperature 300° F.

Remove from fire, add the butter and the chopped, salted popped corn. Stir only enough to mix well. Too much stirring will cause the brittle to "sugar." Turn quickly on a greased slab or on greased inverted pans or baking sheets. Do not scrape the saucepan, as this may cause the brittle to "sugar."

Have enough pans to give space for the brittle to be poured out in very thin sheets.

Smooth out with a spatula. After about one-half minute take hold of the edges of the candy and lifting it slightly from the slab, pull it as thin as possible. If the candy is on a large sheet it may be necessary to break off the thin pieces at the edges in order to pull the center.

Break into irregular pieces.

Cold water test when candy reaches 300° F.: brittle.

Yield (large recipe): weight—one and one-half pounds.

**Amber Pop Corn.**—Follow the directions for pop corn crisp, using unchopped, popped corn.

Turn the cooked candy out on a greased slab or on greased inverted pans or baking sheets.

Pull the brittle into small pieces, having about five grains of popped corn stuck together to form each piece. Each grain should be well covered with this coating and there should not be spaces of clear candy between the grains of popped corn.

## "JOHNNY CAKE"

| LARGE RECIPE | SMALL RECIPE |
|---|---|
| Popped corn, chopped before measuring, 1½ cups | Popped corn, chopped before measuring, ¾ cup |
| Shelled peanuts, ½ cup | Shelled peanuts, ¼ cup |
| Brown sugar, 1½ cups | Brown sugar, ¾ cup |
| Light corn syrup, ½ cup | Light corn syrup, ¼ cup |
| Water, ¾ cup | Water, ½ cup |
| Molasses, 2 tablespoons | Molasses, 1 tablespoon |
| Butter, 2 tablespoons | Butter, 1 tablespoon |
| Soda, ¼ teaspoon | Soda, ⅛ teaspoon |
| Salt, ½ teaspoon | Salt, ¼ teaspoon |

Brown the peanuts in the oven and break them into pieces. Chop the popped corn in a chopping bowl. It should be quite coarse.

Put the sugar, corn syrup, and water into a saucepan and cook, stirring, until the sugar is dissolved. Continue cooking, until the temperature 270° F. is reached. Add the molasses and butter and cook, stirring constantly to prevent scorching, to 275° F.

Remove from fire, add soda (free from lumps), and stir until it ceases to bubble. Add chopped, popped corn and nuts, mixed with the salt, and stir until well mixed. If using the large recipe have the corn warm. Turn into small, greased patty tins, making cakes one-fourth of an inch thick. On top of each little cake place a half peanut. When cold remove from the pans.

It is necessary to work rapidly when turning the mixture into the pans, as it hardens very quickly. If it begins to become hard it is better to set the saucepan of candy into a pan of hot water while dipping out the cakes.

Cold water test when the candy reaches 270° F.: hard, almost brittle.

Yield (large recipe): number of cakes—thirty-two (one and one-fourth inches in diameter and one-fourth of an inch thick).

## SUGARED POP CORN

| LARGE RECIPE | SMALL RECIPE |
|---|---|
| Sugar, 1 cup | Sugar, ½ cup |
| Water, ¾ cup | Water, ½ cup |
| Coloring, pink | Coloring, pink |
| Confectioners' sugar, 3 tablespoons | Confectioners' sugar, 1½ tablespoons |
| Popped corn, 2½ quarts | Popped corn, 5 cups |

Cook together the sugar and the water until the temperature 238° F. is reached, stirring only until the sugar is dissolved.

Remove from fire and add pink coloring paste which has been dissolved in a teaspoon of water. Stir enough to mix the coloring through the syrup.

Have the popped corn in a large bowl so that when the syrup is added there will be room enough for thorough mixing. Pour the syrup slowly over the popped corn, which has previously been slightly salted. Stir the corn during this addition so that each grain may be completely coated with the syrup. Sprinkle the corn with the confectioners' sugar, continuing the stirring, until the syrup "sugars." Turn the corn out on a greased slab or on waxed paper and separate the grains.

Cold water test when syrup reaches 238° F.: soft ball.

Yield (large recipe): two and one-half quarts.

## CHOCOLATE POP CORN

| LARGE RECIPE | SMALL RECIPE |
|---|---|
| Sugar, 1½ cups | Sugar, ¾ cup |
| Light corn syrup, ½ cup | Light corn syrup, ¼ cup |
| Water, ¾ cup | Water, ½ cup |
| Butter, 3 tablespoons | Butter, 1½ tablespoons |
| Chocolate, 3 squares (3 ounces) | Chocolate, 1½ squares (1½ ounces) |
| Popped corn, 3 quarts | Popped corn, 1½ quarts |
| Confectioners' sugar, 2 tablespoons | Confectioners' sugar, 1 tablespoon |

Cook together the sugar, corn syrup, and water, stirring until the sugar is dissolved. While the syrup is cooking melt the chocolate over hot water. When the syrup reaches 270° F. remove from the fire, add the butter and the melted chocolate, and stir until thoroughly mixed.

Pour in a thin stream over the popped corn which has been slightly salted. Stir the corn during the addition of the chocolate syrup so that each grain may be completely coated. Sprinkle the corn with the confectioners' sugar, continuing the stirring until the syrup "sugars." Turn out on a greased slab or on waxed paper, and separate the grains.

Cold water test when syrup reaches 270° F.: hard, almost brittle.

Yield (large recipe): three quarts.

## MAPLE SUGAR POP CORN

| LARGE RECIPE | SMALL RECIPE |
|---|---|
| Maple sugar, 1½ cups | Maple sugar, ¾ cup |
| Water, 1 cup | Water, ¾ cup |
| Popped corn, 2½ quarts | Popped corn, 5 cups |
| Confectioners' sugar, 3 tablespoons | Confectioners' sugar, 1½ tablespoons |

Add the water to the maple sugar and cook, stirring only until the sugar is dissolved.  Continue cooking until the temperature 238° F. is reached.  Remove from fire and pour the syrup slowly over the popped corn, which has previously been slightly salted.  Stir the corn during this addition so that each grain will be completely coated with the syrup.  Sprinkle the corn with the confectioners' sugar, continuing the stirring until the syrup "sugars."

Turn the corn out on a greased slab or on waxed paper and separate the grains.

Cold water test when syrup reaches 238° F.: soft ball.

Yield (large recipe): two and one-half quarts.

# Chapter 16:

## NUTS

Nut candies are popular because the nuts add flavor and relieve the sweetness of the candy. Pecans, almonds, and walnuts are the varieties mentioned most often in our recipes, because these are the nuts most commonly found in markets. However, other nuts may be substituted for them.

**Freshening Nuts.**—The flavor of almost all nuts is improved by heating them for a few minutes in a moderate oven until they become crisp. For some recipes the nuts should be left in the oven until they are delicately browned. This browning brings out the flavor and is desirable wherever it is not necessary to keep the light color.

If the nuts are slightly rancid they should be covered with boiling water, allowed to stand for about three minutes, drained, dried on a clean tea towel, and put into the oven to become crisp.

NUTS IN THE SHELL AND OUT

| KIND OF NUTS | WEIGHT IN SHELL | WEIGHT OF SHELLED NUT MEATS | MEASURE OF SHELLED NUT MEATS |
|---|---|---|---|
| Almonds .......... | 1 pound | 7 ounces | 1⅓ cups |
| English walnuts ... | 1 pound | 7¼ ounces | 2 cups |
| Pecans ........... | 1 pound | 7 ounces | 2 cups |
| Peanuts .......... | 1 pound | 11 ounces | 1¾ cups |

**Blanching Nuts.**—Almonds and pistachio nuts are commonly blanched to remove the dark outer skin. To blanch nuts, cover with boiling water, and allow to stand until the skins loosen. Drain off the hot water and plunge the nuts into cold water. The skins can be easily rubbed off.

Do not try to blanch too many nuts at a time. If the nuts remain too long in the water they become soaked. If they are removed from the water and stand before having their skins rubbed off, they become dry and the skins stick.

Almonds should always be dried in the oven after being blanched. Pistachio nuts should never be put in the oven after blanching, as the heat spoils their bright green color.

## SALTED NUTS

**Shelled nuts, 1 pound**
**Salad oil,     1 pint**
**Salt**

Almonds and peanuts are commonly salted. However, salted pecans, English walnuts, hazelnuts, pistachio nuts, and Brazil nuts are equally good. For variety, combinations of salted nuts can be served, but each kind must be salted separately, as some brown more quickly than others.

Cooking the nuts in oil in a saucepan on top of the stove gives a uniformity of color and crispness. This is very difficult to achieve by cooking them in the oven.

If almonds are to be salted, they should be blanched and dried. Peanuts should have the shells and the red skins removed.

Do not try to put more than one-half cup of nut meats into the oil at one time.

Heat the oil in a small saucepan over a medium flame to the temperature 360°-370° F. Drop in the nuts and stir to keep them from browning on the bottom of the pan. A frying basket gives good results but requires a large amount of oil. Cook until they are a golden brown. A few nuts will have to be lifted out of the oil from time to time, in order to see their true shade. Because of the color of the oil it is difficult to tell the exact shade of the nuts while they are cooking. Do not allow the nuts to become too dark. Especial care must be taken with walnuts and pecans.

When the nuts are a golden brown, remove from the oil and place them on unglazed paper to drain. Transfer to a second sheet of paper and sprinkle with salt.

**Buttered Nuts.**—Prepare nuts as for salting. Place them in a baking pan with butter, allowing one teaspoon of butter to each cup of nuts. Bake in a slow oven from ten to fifteen minutes. They should be crisp and golden brown.

Buttered nuts are especially good for salads or combined with caramel sauce to pour over ice cream.

If almonds are to be buttered, they should be very thoroughly dried in the oven before the butter is added.

**Chocolate Coated Nuts.**—Melt and work dipping chocolate according to directions given in Chapter XVIII.

Any kind of nut may be coated with chocolate, but *all* nuts are improved in flavor if first browned slightly in the oven.

The nuts can be coated singly or arranged in clusters. To form clusters, remove nuts from chocolate, one at a time, and place them on the board so that they will touch each other, and will stick together after the chocolate hardens. The prettiest clusters are formed with three nuts. Because of their shape, hazel nuts are specially attractive.

**Chocolate Acorns.**—Dip the rounded end of a blanched almond into melted chocolate so that about one half of the nut is covered. Take from chocolate and roll in chopped nuts, either pistachio nuts or browned almonds. The chopped nuts cling to the soft chocolate, forming the rough end of the acorn.

### GLACÉ FOR NUTS

| | |
|---|---|
| Sugar, | 1 cup |
| Light corn syrup, | ⅓ cup |
| Water, | ½ cup |

If almonds or pistachio nuts are to be used they should be blanched, and the almonds should be delicately browned in the oven. Freshen other nuts in the oven, if necessary.

Put the sugar, corn syrup, and water into a saucepan and cook, stirring until the sugar is dissolved. Continue the cooking, without stirring, until the temperature 300° F. is reached. As sugar crystals form on the sides of the pan they must be washed away with a wet cloth. This cooking should be done in a small saucepan, and the latter part of the cooking done over a low flame so that the syrup will not discolor. The proper color for a glacé is a delicate straw shade.

When the syrup is done, remove from the fire and set into boiling water to prevent hardening. Drop a few nuts into the syrup. Dip them out, one by one, and place them on a flat, greased surface. The easiest way to dip nuts is to hold a fork in each hand, lift the nut from the syrup with one, and push it from the first fork with the second. Remove as little surplus syrup with the nuts as possible. The glacé should cover the nut, but the base should be only slightly larger than the nut itself.

A superfluous amount of glacé around the base of the nut indicates the work of an amateur. As in chocolate dipping, skill in glacé dipping comes only through practice.

Stir the syrup as little as possible when dipping the nuts, to prevent crystallization.

When the syrup becomes too thick for dipping, it can be reheated, but care must be taken that it does not brown.

If the syrup becomes too firm, it will be necessary to add water and re-cook to the original temperature.

The keeping quality of glacé for nuts is not satisfactory. The best results are obtained when it is made the day it is to be used. If the nuts are to be kept they should be put in layers in a tin box, with waxed paper between the layers, and the box should be tightly closed. Do not put any other kind of candy in with them, as they will absorb the moisture and become sticky.

The glacé can be colored and flavored. Coloring or flavoring should be added just as soon as the syrup is taken from the fire and stirred as little as possible.

## SPICED NUTS

| LARGE RECIPE | SMALL RECIPE |
|---|---|
| Almonds, blanched, ½ pound | Almonds, blanched, ¼ pound |
| Egg white, 1 | Egg white, ½ |
| Water, cold, 1½ tablespoons | Water, cold, 1 tablespoon |
| Confectioners' sugar, 2 cups | Confectioners' sugar, 1 cup |
| Cornstarch, ½ cup | Cornstarch, ¼ cup |
| Salt, 2 teaspoons | Salt, 1 teaspoon |
| Cinnamon, ½ cup | Cinnamon, ¼ cup |
| Ginger, 2 teaspoons | Ginger, 1 teaspoon |
| Cloves, ground, 1 tablespoon | Cloves, ground, ½ tablespoon |
| Nutmeg, ground, 1 teaspoon | Nutmeg, ground, ½ teaspoon |

Blanch the almonds and place in a slow oven to dry. Pecans or walnuts may be used instead of the almonds, or mixed with them. These nuts need not be blanched, but should be freshened in the oven.

Sift the sugar, cornstach, salt, and spices together three times in order to mix thoroughly.

To the egg white add the cold water, and beat slightly so that the egg will not be stringy. Put a portion of the nuts into a coarse strainer and dip up and down in the egg white until each nut is well coated with the egg. Drain.

Roll the nuts in a small amount of the spiced sugar mixture which has been placed on a sheet of paper.

In shallow pans put layers of the spiced sugar mixture about one-fourth of an inch thick. Drop the coated nuts into this, leaving spaces between them. Cover with the spiced sugar mixture.

Bake for three hours in an oven at 250° F. (very slow). This long baking gives the spices opportunity to penetrate the nuts, and also makes the nuts crisp. The finished nuts should be completely covered with a thin, brittle coating of the spiced sugar mixture.

Remove from the oven and sift the sugar from the nuts. Keep the sugar and spice mixture in jars for future use.

**General Directions for Stuffed Prunes.**—Stuffed prunes are being used more and more commonly and often take the place of candy, especially for children.

In selecting the prunes, consider the way in which they are to be used. If in combination with candy, prunes of the smaller sizes (as 40-50s) are more desirable. The big fancy prunes (20-30s) are too large to look dainty in a box of candy, but are usually preferred for a box of stuffed prunes only.

The prunes should be washed and steamed. For steaming, place them in a collander or coarse strainer over a kettle of boiling water, taking care that no water touches the fruit. Cover tightly and allow the steam to soften them for five to ten minutes. The time of steaming depends upon the dryness of the prunes. They should be plump and tender, but not soft, when taken from the steam.

Various mixtures may be used for stuffing prunes, but nuts or mixtures of fruits blend most acceptably with the prune flavor. Fondant alone is too sweet to be interesting.

Whole almonds, blanched and dried, may be put into the prunes. A mixture of chopped almonds and pecans, held together by ground prune pulp, is a good stuffing.

Do not fill the prunes too full because when they are too large they are unappetizing and difficult to eat.

**STUFFED PRUNES I**

| | |
|---|---|
| Prunes, | 15 |
| Candied Apricots, | 6 |
| Almonds, | ¼ cup |

Blanch the almonds and heat them in the oven until a delicate brown. Put the candied apricots and the almonds through the food chopper and knead well together.  If the apricots are dry, add a little orange juice to moisten the mixture.

Wash the prunes, steam them for about five minutes, and remove the seeds.  Stuff with the apricot mixture.  Do not roll in sugar because it detracts from the black, shiny appearance and does not improve the flavor.

### STUFFED PRUNES II

Prunes, 16
Citron, 1 tablespoon
Nut meats, ¼ cup
Raisins, seedless or seeded, ¼ cup

Wash prunes and steam for five minutes.  Remove seeds. Pick over raisins and remove stems.

Put citron, nuts, and raisins through the food chopper. Knead.  Add fruit juice if the mixture is dry.

Stuff prunes.

### STUFFED DATES I

Dates, 30
Figs, 4
Nut meats, ¼ cup
Prunes, 6
Cinnamon, ½ teaspoon
Cloves, ¼ teaspoon

Wash prunes and figs and steam for five minutes.  Remove seeds from the prunes.

Put figs, nuts, and prunes through meat chopper; add spices and mix thoroughly.  If the mixture is too dry, add lemon or orange juice.  Wash and seed dates and fill with fruit mixture.  Roll in granulated sugar.

## STUFFED DATES II

> Dates, 30
> Orange peel, chopped, 2 tablespoons
> Cocoanut, ¼ cup
> Dates, 9 (put through food chopper)

Scrape white inner skin from orange peel. Wash and dry dates and remove seeds.

Put cocoanut, nine dates, and orange peel through the food chopper. Orange juice may be added if the mixture is dry.

Fill the thirty dates with the fruit mixture and roll them in granulated sugar.

## VARIOUS STUFFED FRUITS

**Stuffed Cherries.**—Candied cherries may be stuffed with nuts, fondant, almond paste, or fruit mixtures.

Open the cherry by making two cuts, with a sharp knife, cutting halfway through the cherry, so that four points are formed. When the cherry is stuffed these points will come up around the stuffing like petals.

A whole blanched almond can be inserted in the cherry, making an acorn-shaped confection. The cherry may be rolled in tiny colored candies, which will adhere to the cherry, but not to the nut.

Fondant, mixed with nuts, or nuts and candied apricots, may be used as stuffing. Butter fondant is especially good.

The fruit mixture used in stuffed prunes I (page 122), is tart enough to blend well with the cherry flavor.

Almond paste, mixed with fondant in the proportion of two measures of paste to one of fondant, may be used for the cherry stuffing. Suggestions for decorations are given in Chapter XIX, Decorative Sweets for the Candy Box.

**Stuffed Figs.**—Wash the figs and steam them, according to the general directions given under stuffed prunes (page 122).

Cut in half. Open with a sharp knife, and stuff. A whole fig is too large when stuffed.

The fruit confection mixture (see below) is a good type to put into the centers of the figs, but variations can be made according to the fruits and nuts available.

**Stuffed Raisins.**—Seeded raisins should be picked over and steamed for about three minutes. The steaming should be done only long enough to soften them and make them plump. The time will depend upon the dryness of the fruit. (For directions for steaming, see stuffed prunes, page 122.)

Open the raisins with a sharp pointed knife, making a lengthwise slit. Stuff with pieces of nut, ground fruit (such as the mixture for stuffed prunes I, page 122), fondant, or almond paste. The fondant or almond paste may be colored delicate pink or green to contrast with the dark color of the raisins.

Raisins with colored stuffings may be coated with glacé and used effectively as decorations for dishes of bonbons.

A small cluster from a bunch of raisins may be stuffed. Steam; remove the seeds carefully so that the raisins will not be loosened from the stems; stuff the raisins with bits of fondant or almond paste of different shades.

## FRUIT PASTE

Prunes, uncooked, ½ cup
Figs, ¼ cup
Raisins, ½ cup
Dates, ½ cup
Nut meats, ¼ cup
Salt, ¼ teaspoon
Ground cloves, ¼ teaspoon

Wash figs and prunes and steam for five minutes. Remove seeds from raisins, dates, and prunes. Put fruit and nuts through food chopper. Add salt and cloves and mix well together. Fruit juices can be added if the mixture seems dry.

Roll out in a sheet one-fourth of an inch thick. Cut into

squares or diamonds or into fancy shapes with cutters. Sprinkle with confectioners' sugar. Shake to remove super-fluous sugar. Other spices, as ginger and cinnamon, may be used in combination with the cloves.

Yield: number of pieces—sixty; weight—two-thirds of a pound.

## APRICOT PASTE

> Dried apricots, ¾ cup
> Lemon juice, 1 tablespoon
> Desiccated cocoanut, ¾ cup
> Nut meats, chopped, ½ cup
> Grated orange rind, ½ teaspoon
> Grated lemon rind, ½ teaspoon

Wash apricots and steam for about five minutes. Put nuts, cocoanut, and apricots through food chopper. Add lemon juice and rind, and orange rind, and knead until well blended. If mixture is very dry add orange juice to moisten it. Roll out in a sheet one-fourth of an inch thick. Cut into small squares or diamonds or into fancy shapes with cutters.

Yield: number of pieces—sixty; weight—nine ounces.

## SPICED RAISINS

| LARGE RECIPE | SMALL RECIPE |
|---|---|
| Raisins, 1 cup | Raisins, ½ cup |
| Sugar, 1½ cups | Sugar, ¾ cup |
| Water, 1 cup | Water, ¾ cup |
| Cinnamon, 1 teaspoon | Cinnamon, ½ teaspoon |
| Nutmeg, ¼ teaspoon | Nutmeg, ⅛ teaspoon |
| Cloves, ground, ½ teaspoon | Cloves, ground, ¼ teaspoon |
| Ginger, ½ teaspoon | Ginger, ¼ teaspoon |
| Sugar for rolling the raisins | Sugar for rolling the raisins |

Seeded or unseeded raisins may be used. Pick them over carefully, removing stems.

Put the sugar, water, and spices into a saucepan and cook,

stirring until the sugar is dissolved. Continue cooking, without stirring, until the temperature 238° F. is reached. Add raisins and cook slowly for about seven minutes, stirring only enough to separate the raisins and keep the syrup from scorching.

Remove from the fire. Set into a pan of hot water. Take a few raisins at a time from the syrup, drain, and drop into granulated sugar. Separate at once and roll each raisin until well covered with sugar.

The attractiveness of the fruit depends upon having the raisins well drained and keeping each raisin separated from the others.

Should the mixture of raisins and syrup become sugary before all are dipped out, add about one-fourth of a cup of water and recook. In recooking heat slowly at first, until all the sugar is dissolved; then cook for about five minutes until the syrup is thickened.

### CANDIED ORANGE PEEL

Peel of 4 medium-sized oranges
Sugar, 2 cups
Water in which orange peel has been cooked, 1 cup

With the point of a sharp knife, cut through the peel of the orange so that it can be removed in quarters. Cover with cold water, bring to the boiling point, and cook slowly until soft.

Drain, saving the water for making the syrup. Scrape out the white inner portion of the peel with a teaspoon. With the scissors, cut the yellow skin into thin strips.

To the sugar add one cup of the water in which the orange peel was cooked. Should there be less than a cup of this liquid, add water to make up the measure. Boil to the temperature 238° F. (soft ball in cold water). Add the orange peel and cook slowly for ten minutes or longer until most of the water has evaporated. Drain in a coarse sieve. Drop the orange peel, a few pieces at a time, in a pan containing a layer of granulated sugar. Separate the pieces with forks. Roll until each piece is completely covered with sugar. Shake off any excess sugar.

**Candied Grapefruit or Lemon Peel.**—Candied grapefruit peel can be prepared in the same way as the orange peel. Because of the size of the grapefruit, its peel should be removed in six sections instead of four.

It is better to use fresh water for the syrup, as the grapefruit peel gives the water in which it has been cooked a bitter flavor.

In cooking the syrup for the lemon peel, use fresh water and add six or seven whole cloves.

## GLACÉ FOR FRUITS

> Sugar, 1 cup
> Light corn syrup, ⅓ cup
> Water, ½ cup

Put the sugar, water, and corn syrup into a saucepan and cook, stirring until the sugar is dissolved. Continue the cooking, without stirring, until the temperature 300° F. is reached. If sugar crystals form on the sides of the pan they must be washed away with a wet cloth. The cooking should be done in a small saucepan, and over a low flame during the latter part, so that the syrup will not discolor. The proper color for a glacé is a delicate straw shade.

When the syrup is done, remove from the fire and set the saucepan into boiling water to prevent the syrup from hardening. Dip the pieces of fruit, one at a time, into the syrup; remove them and place on a greased, flat surface.

On account of the juice in the fruit, the glacé softens quickly and must be made the day it is to be used.

In dipping, do not stick a fork or skewer into the fruit, because this will cause the juice to flow.

Tangerines should be peeled and separated into sections,

and care taken not to break the membrane enclosing each section. Remove all the strings of white inner skin, lay the sections one at a time on a fork, and dip quickly into the glacé.

Small pieces of preserved pineapple or candied cherries or apricots can be coated with the glacé.

Strawberries should be held by the stem when being dipped into the glacé.

Cut white grapes from the bunch, leaving a short piece of stem. Hold by this stem when dipping into the glacé.

## APPLE ON A STICK

Sugar, 2 cups
Light corn syrup, ½ cup
Water, ¾ cup
Red coloring, few drops
Red apples, 12
Skewers, 12
Flavoring oil, few drops

The wooden skewers can be purchased from the butcher. Wash the apples thoroughly and dry them. Insert the skewer in the blossom end.

Put the sugar, corn syrup, and water into a saucepan and cook, stirring until the sugar is dissolved. Continue cooking, without stirring, until the temperature 300° F. is reached. During the cooking any sugar crystals thrown on the sides of the pan should be washed away with a wet cloth. The latter part of the cooking should be done slowly so that the syrup will not darken.

Remove the syrup from the fire and set the saucepan at once into boiling water so that it will not cool and thicken. It is convenient to use a small double boiler for this, the upper part for cooking the syrup and the lower part filled with boiling water to keep the syrup hot. The utensil for cooking should be of a shape to allow the syrup to be deep enough to cover the whole apple.

Add coloring and stir enough to mix well. The syrup should be a bright red. Oil of peppermint, clove, or cinnamon may be added for flavoring.

Holding the apple by the skewer, plunge it into the hot syrup. Draw it out quickly and twirl it until the syrup runs down to the stick and spreads smoothly over the apple. Stand the skewer in a small rack or vase so that the apple does not touch anything while hardening. A rack can be improvised with a cake cooler, or a piece of wire fencing.

These apples should be made the day they are to be used because the moisture from the apple will soften the candy and make it sticky.

The dipping must be done rapidly or the syrup will become too stiff for coating.

Cold water test when the candy reaches 300° F.: very brittle.

## SALTED RAISINS

| LARGE RECIPE | SMALL RECIPE |
|---|---|
| Raisins, 2 cups | Raisins, 1 cup |
| Salad oil, 1 cup | Salad oil, ¾ cup |
| Salt | Salt |

Either seeded or seedless raisins can be used. Large raisins look more attractive when served. Clean the raisins and remove stems and bits of seed.

Heat the oil to 370° F. Drop in the raisins a few at a time, and cook slowly until they are plump. Remove from oil and drain on unglazed paper. Transfer to a clean paper and sprinkle with salt. Shake to remove superfluous salt.

These are appropriate for afternoon tea, as well as for use as an after-dinner confection.

**Devilled Raisins.**—These are prepared as the salted raisins, with a shake of cayenne mixed with the salt and sprinkled over the cooked raisins. Be careful not to add too much cayenne or the raisins will be too hot.

# Chapter 18:

## CHOCOLATE DIPPING

**General Directions.**—Chocolate dipping is difficult. In the candy business it is considered a trade and girls work from two to three years before they become expert dippers. Small wonder then that the homemade chocolate creams which appear at candy sales or bazaars look so different from the commercial products!

Caramels, nougat, fudge, kisses—countless homemade candies such as these—even on the first trial, can successfully compete with those of the confectioner. But homemade chocolates must be tried many times before even passable results are acquired, and if you are not willing to spend this time gaining skill, it is better to make the other kinds of candy and buy your chocolates.

The chief advantage in dipping chocolates at home is that you can have the kinds of centers you like best.

There are difficulties besides lack of technique. It is often hard to secure the right kind of coating-chocolate. This is specially prepared and is quite a different thing from the bitter chocolate used for cooking. Often dipping-chocolate must be purchased from a confectioner and usually he will not wish to sell less than a ten pound cake.

However, if the demand is sufficient a good grade of dipping-chocolate can be purchased from the grocer in one-half pound cakes. Many of the semi-sweet and milk chocolate bars which are found on all candy counters, may also be used successfully for chocolate dipping.

There are many grades and brands of coating-chocolate. In buying, select a good quality. If you do much chocolate dipping you should have both sweetened and unsweetened chocolate on hand—the former for nuts and fruits, and the latter for sweet centers.

The equipment for chocolate dipping is relatively simple. A small double boiler, a fork or chocolate dipper, and boards or trays are the essential things. The chocolates should be dropped on the covered boards or trays so that they can be removed from the dipping table as soon as they are coated. The covering may be heavy waxed paper, but if you are doing much dipping it will pay you to have boards over which table oilcloth has been stretched and fastened in place. The oilcloth gives the under side of the chocolate the smooth, soft gloss which is desirable.

Do not try to work with less than a pound of chocolate at one time. Two pounds are even better. With a large amount of chocolate it is easier to keep the temperature even. There need be no waste because chocolate which is left over can be remelted and used another time.

Break the chocolate into pieces sufficiently small to melt readily. Put them into the upper part of a double boiler and place over hot water—not above 130° F. Do not have a fire under the water, as you are apt to overheat the chocolate and this is fatal to good dipping. Stir the chocolate constantly while it is melting, so that the chocolate in the bottom of the container, next to the hot water, will not become too hot. Its temperature must *never* go above 110° F.

If you are experienced it is better to dip with a large amount of the melted coating at one time, as it will remain at the desired temperature longer. But if you are inexperienced, you may find it better to take about a cup of the coating from the double boiler, work it until ready for use, dip as many chocolates as possible, and then add fresh chocolate from the double boiler. A small enamel bowl with sloping sides is the most convenient utensil for holding the chocolate while working and dipping.

When the melted coating is taken from the hot water it should be worked constantly until it reaches the proper thickness for coating. Dipping experts always use the hand for this "working." In this way the tiniest lumps can be smoothed out, and after you become experienced you can tell by feeling the chocolate when the time for dipping has come.

Keep warm over water which is at 85° F.

The tests for the right consistency are—temperature 88° to 83° F. and dipping a trial center.

Different kinds and brands of chocolate are ready for use at slightly different temperatures. When placed on the board this coated center should be perfectly smooth, except for the little marking at the top, and should not have a projecting base. It should harden quickly.

Never add water to dipping-chocolate. If it becomes too thick it must be carefully remelted. Water will make it stiff and cause it to lose its gloss.

When the chocolate becomes too cool for coating centers it may be used for making nut or raisin clusters. To do this fill the soft chocolate with nuts or raisins and drop the mixture from the tip of a teaspoon on waxed paper or on the covered board.

The temperature of the room for dipping is quite as important as the temperature of the chocolate. Dipping cannot be done in a warm room. The temperature should never go above 65° F., and 60° F. is even better. In candy factories the temperature of the chocolate room is regulated by brine pipes and the humidity is controlled. When dipping at home, do not have steam in the room.

The finished chocolates should be cooled quickly or light spots will appear when they are dry. If the room is not cold put the trays of chocolates into the refrigerator and leave them there until the coating hardens.

A good arrangement of the dipping table is to have the centers to be coated ready on a tray at the left of the chocolate bowl, and the covered board for the dipped chocolates at the right. The actual dipping can be done with the hands or with a fork. Drop the center into the chocolate; cover completely. Lift from the bowl, scraping excess chocolate from the fork on the side of the bowl. Drop the dipped center on the board. As the candy leaves the fork, or fingers, there will be a little string of chocolate, which by a simple twist becomes the professional-looking mark on the top.

**Centers for Chocolates.**—Nuts are easier to dip than cream centers, hence it is wise for beginners to use them in practicing. Since they are small, it is easier to dip them with a fork than with the hand. Always crisp the nuts in the oven before coating them.

Fondant for centers should be shaped in a long roll. The board for rolling may be sprinkled very lightly with flour or cornstarch. To make the centers uniform in size, cut the roll into four pieces of equal length. Lay these side by side; with a large knife cut the four at once, making from each the same number of pieces, of the same size.

Do not make the centers too large. They will look much larger after they are dipped, and except for nougat, marshmallows, or some special centers, large candies are undesirable.

Be sure to cover each center completely with the chocolate so that not the tiniest place is exposed. If the coating is thin or broken, there will be a "leak." The cream center will ooze out, forming a sticky spot, and spoil the looks and keeping qualities of the candy.

Dipping is easier if the centers are the shape of the old-fashioned chocolate creams—rounding peaks. These can be made by rolling the pieces of fondant into balls, and then shaping them.

For home work, centers should be dipped soon after shaping. The centers become softer after being coated, but if they have become too dry while standing they will never be of the desired creamy consistency. The fondant may be made some time before it is needed and kept in a covered jar until shaping is to be done.

The softest, creamiest centers are those made from oriental

creams. These are an exception to the general rule, in that they should be made the same day they are to be dipped. If allowed to stand they become too soft for shaping.

**Suggestions for Centers.**—Centers can be made from almost any candy or nuts. Fondant may be colored and flavored to suit the fancy, for soft centers. Hard centers may be made from caramels, nougat, butterscotch, butter crunch, nuts, or preserved fruits, singly or in combinations.

## Chapter 19:

### DECORATIVE SWEETS FOR THE CANDY BOX

Every once in a while we want to pack a box of candy for a gift or a sale, or arrange a dish of assorted sweets for a party, and we long to have our work compare favorably with that of the confectioner. Usually our standard of quality is high but the homemade candies lack the professional touch which lends color and life to the box.

This touch can be given without unusual or expensive ingredients if you use imagination, patience, and time. The box acquires distinction and charm by careful packing and by the addition of out-of-the-ordinary accessories, decorated or tinted candies, stuffed fruits with centers of contrasting colors, and brightly wrapped bonbons.

Most of these decorative sweets do not require new recipes —merely adaptations of those already given.

**Chocolate Accessories.**—Melt dipping-chocolate and prepare it for use, according to directions given (page 132). Pour from the tip of a teaspoon, forming small drops. These should be dropped on the oilcloth-covered boards used for chocolate dipping or on a slightly greased slab or inverted pan. The chocolate must be well worked for these drops, just as for dipping, or the candies will streak. It should be cool enough to hold its shape when dropped. Before the drops harden sprinkle thickly with tiny silver or colored candies, which can be purchased from a confectioner.

Sweet dipping chocolate can be melted, worked, and poured into tiny molds of fancy shapes. Remove from molds when cold and put into the boxes to give a touch of dark color in a layer of light candies, or wrap in silver, gold, or colored tin foil to form a contrast with dark candies.

136

Chocolate acorns, especially those dipped in chopped pistachio nuts, give a touch of bright color. (Directions for making are given on page 119). These and spiced raisins are useful as chink fillers, when boxes are to be packed tightly for shipping.

**Decorated Fondant Patties.**—Follow directions for making fondant patties (page 29). While these are still soft, press into them bits of candied fruit or bright candies forming designs. A flowering plant can be made with a raisin or cherry for its pot, a stem and leaves of angelica or pistachio nut, and flowers of tiny, colored candies.

A single flower can be made with shredded, blanched almonds for petals, a round yellow candy for a center, and a green stem of angelica. This is effective on a delicately tinted patty where the white of the almond shows to advantage.

For the children, funny faces can be drawn on the patties with a tooth pick dipped into melted chocolate.

A butterfly can be made with a body of a caraway comfit and wings cut from pieces of fruit.

Bright candies of contrasting colors, sprinkled on the patties with a careful carelessness, add to their effectiveness.

**Marzipan.**—The name marzipan is given to candies with a foundation of almond paste. These are usually tinted and shaped in the form of tiny fruits, flowers, or vegetables.

The almond paste can be bought from the confectioner and mixed with an equal amount of vanilla fondant. This makes it of a good consistency for molding and less concentrated in flavor.

Color some of the marzipan a delicate yellow. Mold it in the shape of a small pear, making the stem and the blossom end of cloves. With a brush, tint one side of the pear a soft pink.

In a similar manner various fruits and vegetables can be fashioned. Some of the simplest to make are carrots, bananas, peas in the pod, green string beans, and pumpkins.

With even a limited skill, flowers can be made. If small

balls of marzipan are colored different shades, they can be effectively shaped and combined to form sweet peas, rose buds, or violets.

Two halves of pecans can be fastened together with a small piece of colored marzipan. These are much prettier when glacé covered.

**Decorated Stuffed Fruits.**—One of the most effective finishing touches for the candy box is decorated stuffed fruit. A dark prune with a light colored stuffing—tinted marzipan or butter fondant—upon which is placed a wee marzipan rosebud or violet, will be the center of interest in a dish of bonbons. The decorations on the stuffing need not be so difficult as the marzipan flowers. Conventional designs may be worked out with candied cherries, bits of angelica or pistachio nuts, or bright little candies. The prune may be made to look like a dark basket of flowers by putting a handle made from a strip of prune or cherry across the center of the stuffing, and making little flower designs at the ends. The simplest designs, with a touch of red candied cherry and green pistachio nuts on the fruit stuffing, are in many cases as attractive as the more elaborate ones.

Stuffed dates can be decorated in the same way as the prunes. Even the small raisin can have a stuffing of pink marzipan contrasting with its dark color and a small ball of silver candy or a caraway comfit stuck in the center.

Stuffed cherries, described on page 124, give a real splash of color.

**Decorated Cakes.**—Rich fruit cake can be cut into cubes of a size to correspond with that of the box to be filled, coated with fondant (page 32) and decorated; or frosted and decorated with ornamental frosting (page 154). This is unusually nice for the center of a box because it helps to keep the candies in place.

These cakes can be decorated to suit the type of box and the season of the year. For Christmas the clear hard candies colored red and green can be broken into tiny bits and sprin-

kled over the top or put on in a holly design. A little plant
in a pot similar to that suggested for the fondant patty (page
137) is effective. The cake can be cut in pieces as small as a
caramel or piece of nougat, dipped in softly tinted fondant
and sprinkled with tiny silver candies.

**Fruits and Nuts Coated with Glacé.**—Glacé adds greatly
to the appearance of a box, but it is quickly softened by the
moisture of other candies. It should never be put into a box
for shipment with other candies and should not be included
in any box which is to be kept for longer than a day.

Glacé gives variety and interest to dishes of bonbons and
can be safely included, if the candy is to be served within a
short time.

**Petites.**—Use the recipe for spiced hard candies (page
89). Color the cooked syrup bright red or green and add
some distinctive flavor, as cinnamon, lime, or clove. Set the
saucepan of candy in a pan of hot water and with a teaspoon
drop very small portions of the candy on a greased slab, inverted pan, or platter. If dropped from the tip of the spoon
these will form perfect rounds and should be made smaller
than a dime. While still warm these can be sprinkled with
tiny, bright-colored candies, caraway comfits, or chopped,
blanched pistachio nuts.

**Hearts and Crescents.**—From the petite mixture any number of fancy shapes can be made, if you have assorted molds.
Small pans in the shapes of hearts or crescents may be slightly
greased and filled with the hot candy. This should be shaken
out as soon as cold, because if it is allowed to harden it may
break upon being removed from the molds.

*Chapter 20:*

# THE CANDY BOX

Have you ever analyzed an attractive box of candy and taken note of the many accessories which make it so tempting? There is the outer wrapping of glazed white paper, smoothly folded, the box itself, tied with ribbon and ornamented with a rosette, then the lacy border and dainty doily, perhaps a layer of glistening paper giving an intriguing glimpse within, and finally the candy itself.

Much effort goes into making the top layer attractive. The candies are arranged carefully and artistically and touches of color are given by bonbons, fruits, and bright pieces of tin foil. So that the box will look as well when you open it as when it leaves the confectioner, care is taken in packing. Sometimes the candies are kept separate by being placed in tiny fluted paper dishes; sometimes they are kept in place by gilt-edged cardboard partitions.

It may not be possible to have all of these elaborate finishings for the home-packed box, but with a little forethought and a small expenditure of money and time, you can make your box look more attractive and professional than the average one packed at home.

It is generally easier to buy boxes of tin than those of pasteboard. Small ones of different colors and shapes can often be found at the ten-cent stores and can be stenciled at home, if you have ability along this line. Colorful gifts can be made by covering pasteboard boxes with bright paper or figured wall paper. A coat of shellac will add to their looks and make them more durable. Plain white boxes tied with ribbons of pastel shades, or with bright colors for the holiday season are always good-looking.

The ribbon can be cut into two pieces of uneven length

and each of these pasted on the inside of the cover on opposite sides of the box and diagonally across from each other, so that they can be brought over the top and tied in a bow or rosette. If the ribbon is arranged in this way the bow will not have to be untied every time the box is opened.

The box should be lined with waxed paper. This can be purchased in rolls or packages. It is inexpensive and is a real necessity for box packing. There should be a piece of waxed paper between the layers of candy and another to cover the top. More effective than the waxed paper for the top covering is the transparent paper, because it is so clear and shining that it seems to add luster to the candies and bring out their colors. However, it is sometimes hard to find and is difficult to keep on hand because it wrinkles easily, and when crushed cannot be pressed.

Lace paper doilies add much to the beauty of the box and, being inexpensive, they should be considered essential. If you cannot find a doily which exactly fits your box, a large square one can be cut the right size and shape.

The paper lace for inside the top of the box can be bought by the yard at the ten-cent store. Instead of these lace strips, gold or silver tin foil can be cut in scallops and put around the box, forming a truly gorgeous border. If this is done the strip of tin foil must be wide enough to extend into the bottom of the box so that it will stay in place. With a large round or oval box, a piece of waxed paper, folded so that it is as wide as the box is deep, can be placed around the inside of the box next to the tin foil. This keeps the tin foil from slipping and protects it from the candy.

Oftentimes cardboard partitions will make the artistic arrangement of candy easier. These should be cut the exact length or width of the box and the desired depth of the layer. Where two strips cross, if an incision is made in each one, they can be fitted together smoothly. For a large box four partitions may divide the top layer into nine compartments.

But for a shallow box two partitions extending from corner to corner make four attractive triangular spaces.

In arranging the candy in a box, fill the bottom layer with the firmer and heavier candies, such as nougat and caramels, or large squares of fudge and slices of caramel nut rolls. These can be packed tightly together and are not crushed by the candies above.

The top layer should show your assortment of candies—at least one piece of each kind you have made. These should be arranged to fit into the layer firmly and show to advantage, with contrasting colors next to each other. To add atmosphere, bright or decorated candies should be interspersed, but unless the box is large do not put in too many fancy confections, as they detract from each other. Some interesting additions are stuffed and decorated prunes and dates, ornamented patties, brightly wrapped candies and bonbons, or nuts coated with delicately tinted fondant.

The rest of the layer can be made up of candies which might be crushed if placed in the bottom and the chinks can be filled with spiced raisins, chocolate acorns, or dipped nuts. (For suggestions for decorative sweets for the candy box, see Chapter XIX.)

It is possible to pack a box which children will love and which will be welcomed not only by them but by their mothers. A small paper cup such as is used for salted nuts can be covered with gold or silver tin foil and filled with raisins. Pulled mints or small pieces of molasses candy may be wrapped and used for filling corners. Prunes, stuffed with the ground fruit mixture and decorated with bright bits of cherry, are both good-looking and healthful. But the crowning joy will be the animals and the lollypops. Animal crackers may be coated with chocolate or with fondant. Those fondant-coated may be decorated with melted chocolate so that Mary's lamb will have a ribbon around its neck and the lion can have a tawny mane. The leopard can accumulate chocolate spots and a chocolate horse is almost dark enough to be called Black Beauty.  The lollypops can have the most extraordinary faces—pirates, clowns, and savages.

Fruits and nuts are sometimes a welcome change from candy.  The box best suited for these is a shallow one, holding but one layer and divided by partitions.  In the center a decorated fruit cake will give color and glamor.  Spiced nuts and raisins can fill two compartments; salted pecans and almonds, two more.  Candied grapefruit, orange, and lemon peel are tart enough to add zest, and stuffed figs, prunes, and raisins will give variety.

## COOKED FROSTINGS

Cooked frostings are of two types: those which are like fudge and those which contain egg white and which are fluffy as well as creamy. The ones which have the egg white are perhaps easier to use as they harden less quickly and thus allow more time for spreading the frosting. However, if any cooked frosting begins to harden so that it crumbs and does not spread with a smooth surface water may be added a little at a time and beaten in to soften the frosting and to restore the gloss.

As in making candy the corn syrup or cream of tartar must be measured accurately for too much of either will cause the frosting to be soft and will make long beating necessary to dry it out.

Egg whites may be beaten with a rotary beater but the frosting itself is heavy and is more easily beaten if a wire whip or a wooden spoon is used.

## HOW TO FROST A CAKE

When the cake is removed from the pan place it with the top crust up on a cooling rack and allow it to cool. Brush off any crumbs which may be clinging to it. Frost the cake on a cake plate or on the cooling rack and remove it to a plate after the frosting has hardened. Spread the frosting as thickly as desired over the bottom layer. Place the second layer over this and lightly press the two together. Scrape the rest of the frosting onto the center of the top layer. Using a spatula or a case knife pull the frosting down over the sides and, using long strokes, spread it evenly around the cake.

Now spread the top smoothly and if a swirl is desired take long, swift strokes around or back and forth making the depressions as deep as the frosting will allow.

## SUGGESTIONS FOR DECORATING CAKES

**Colored Frostings.**—Any one of the white frostings may be delicately tinted by adding a few drops of coloring matter. Add the color when the frosting is just beginning to hold up in peaks and beat it in well, being careful not to add too much for only a delicately tinted cake is attractive.

**Nuts.**—Chopped nuts are very effective as a garnish. They are attractive when used on a background of chocolate, sea foam or even a plain white icing. Chop the nuts finely and sprinkle them on the cake immediately after frosting, pressing them in very gently if necessary. They may be used to cover the top of the cake, to cover the sides only or they may be used to give a ring on the outer rim of the top.

Cup cakes may be treated in the same way. Whole nuts or a combination of nuts and candied fruits may be used to produce a planned design. At Christmas halves of candied cherries and blanched pistachio nuts or small leaf shapes cut from angelica arranged in a holly design make the cake very festive.

**Cocoanut.**—For a fresh or dried cocoanut cake use any one of the recipes for white frosting. Cocoanut may be sprinkled over the frosting between the layers as well as over the top or top and sides of the frosted cake. Fresh cocoanut is very moist and requires that the frosting be drier than when desiccated cocoanut is used.

**Chocolate Coating for Shadow Cake.**—Frost a cake with white frosting making it as smooth as possible on top. Pour one of the following chocolate coating mixtures on the center of the top of the cake letting it run down over the sides, and set it aside to cool.

## CHOCOLATE COATING I

Chocolate, 2 ounces
Butter, 1 tablespoon

Melt the chocolate and butter together and pour over the cake.

## CHOCOLATE COATING II

Semi-sweet chocolate, 4 ounces

Melt the semi-sweet chocolate over hot water. Pour onto top of cake, spread thinly to edge and allow it to run down over edge of cake.

## BOILED FROSTING I

Sugar, 2½ cups                Water, ½ cup
Corn syrup, 5 tablespoons     Egg whites, 2
Vanilla, 1½ teaspoons

Cook together the sugar, corn syrup and water to 242° F. (firm ball in cold water). Remove from the fire and beat the egg whites until stiff but not dry. Pour the syrup slowly into the beaten egg whites, beating during the addition. Add vanilla and continue beating until the mixture will hold its shape. Spread quickly on the cake.

Yield: Enough for tops and sides of three 9-inch layers.

## BOILED FROSTING II

Sugar, 2½ cups                Water, 1 cup
Cream of tartar, ¼ teaspoon   Egg whites, 2
Vanilla, 1½ teaspoons

Cook together the sugar, cream of tartar and water to 242° F. (firm ball in cold water). Allow the syrup to stand undisturbed and beat the egg whites until stiff.  Pour the syrup slowly into the beaten egg whites, beating during the addition.  Add vanilla and continue beating until the frosting will hold its shape.  Spread quickly on the cake.

Yield: Enough for tops and sides of three 9-inch layers.


## BOILED FROSTING III

(This is a very heavy frosting which is suitable for loaf cakes)

| | |
|---|---|
| Sugar, 2½ cups | Water, ½ cup |
| Light corn syrup, ½ cup | Egg whites, 2 |
| Vanilla, 1½ teaspoons | |

Cook together the sugar, corn syrup and water to 242° F. (firm ball in cold water).  Allow the syrup to stand undisturbed and beat the egg whites until stiff.  Pour the syrup slowly into the beaten egg whites, beating during the addition. Add vanilla and continue beating until the frosting will hold its shape.  Spread quickly on the cake.

Yield: Enough for two loaf cakes or one cake baked in a tube pan.


## QUICK COOKED FROSTING

| | |
|---|---|
| Sugar, 1½ cups | Water, ⅓ cup |
| Corn syrup, 1 tablespoon | Egg whites, 2 |
| | Vanilla, 1 teaspoon |

Put the unbeaten egg whites, sugar, corn syrup and water in the top of a double boiler and set over boiling water.  Beat the mixture with a rotary egg beater until the frosting will hold up in peaks (about 7 minutes).  Add the vanilla and beat it in.  Spread quickly on the cake.

Yield: Enough for the tops and sides of two 9-inch layers.

## MARSHMALLOW FROSTING

**One recipe of Quick Cooked Frosting with the vanilla reduced to ½ teaspoon**
  Marshmallows, 2 ounces (8)

When the quick cooked frosting is beginning to hold up in peaks add the marshmallows which were cut into quarters. Continue beating until the frosting will hold its shape. Spread quickly on the cake.

  Yield: Enough for the tops and sides of two 9-inch layers.

## SEA FOAM FROSTING

| | |
|---|---|
| **Light brown sugar, 2½ cups** | **Egg whites, 2** |
| **Water, ½ cup** | **Vanilla, 1 teaspoon** |

Boil the sugar and water together to 252° F. (very firm ball in cold water). Remove from the fire and beat the egg whites until stiff. Add the hot syrup slowly, beating during the addition. Add vanilla and beat until frosting will hold its shape. Spread quickly on cake.

  Yield: Enough for tops and sides of two 9-inch layers.

## FUDGE FROSTING

| | |
|---|---|
| **Sugar, 3 cups** | **Milk, 1 cup** |
| **Light corn syrup, 3 tablespoons** | **Chocolate, 4 ounces** |
| **Butter, ⅓ cup** | **Vanilla, 1 teaspoon** |

Break the chocolate into small pieces. Put the chocolate, sugar, milk and corn syrup into a saucepan and cook slowly, stirring often to prevent scorching, to 232° F. Remove from the fire, add the butter and set aside to cool to 110° F. (lukewarm). Add vanilla and beat until the frosting becomes creamy and barely holds its shape. Spread on cake quickly.

  Yield: Enough to cover the tops and sides of two 9-inch layers.

## CARAMEL FROSTING

Light brown sugar, 3 cups          Butter, ⅓ cup
Top milk, 1 cup                    Vanilla, 1 teaspoon

Put the sugar and milk into a saucepan and cook, stirring frequently, to 234° F. (very soft ball in cold water). Remove from fire, add butter and cool, without stirring, until it is lukewarm (110° F.). Add vanilla and beat until creamy. Spread on cake quickly.

Yield: Enough for tops and sides of two 9-inch layers.


## LADY BALTIMORE FROSTING AND FILLING

(For use with your favorite white cake recipe).

Any white frosting, 1 recipe       Pecans or walnuts, ½ cup,
Raisins, ½ cup, chopped              chopped
Figs, 6, chopped

To the mixed nuts and fruits add enough frosting to make a filling which will spread easily on one layer. Place another layer of cake over this and frost the whole, tops and sides, with the remaining white frosting.


## LORD BALTIMORE FROSTING AND FILLING

(To be used with your favorite gold cake recipe).

Any white frosting, 1 recipe       Pecans, ½ cup, chopped
Macaroon crumbs, 1 cup             Candied cherries, 12
                                   Angelica

To one half the white frosting add the macaroon crumbs and chopped pecans. Spread between layers and on top of cake. Using the remaining white frosting cover the top (over the other frosting) and the sides of the cake.  Garnish with halves of cherries and angelica.

## UNCOOKED AND QUICKLY COOKED FROSTINGS

The popularity of uncooked frostings is due to the fact that they are so quickly and easily made.

The material which gives them body is confectioners' sugar. It is the one best sugar to use because it has the finest grain and gives a smooth frosting which closely resembles a cooked product.

The frostings which contain fats such as butter, chocolate, egg yolk or cream cheese have excellent keeping qualities; in fact, they remain soft and creamy as long as the cake lasts. Those made from confectioners' sugar and a liquid, as fruit juice, dry out more quickly.

It is not always possible to give the exact amount of sugar which will give a frosting of the desired stiffness.  If all of the sugar is not needed, omit some.  If all of the sugar has been added and the frosting is too dry to spread nicely, add extra liquid.  All frostings have more gloss if sufficient liquid is used.

## BITTER SWEET CHOCOLATE FROSTING

| | |
|---|---|
| Butter, 3 tablespoons | Confectioners' sugar, 3 cups |
| Chocolate, 4 ounces | Milk, 6 tablespoons |
| Salt, ⅛ teaspoon | Vanilla, ½ teaspoon |

Melt the butter and the chocolate together.  Add the salt and half of the confectioners' sugar and cream together well. Add the milk in thirds, creaming the mixture after each addition.  Add the rest of the sugar and the vanilla and cream thoroughly.  Spread on a cold cake.

Yield: Enough for tops of two 9-inch layers.

## LIGHT CHOCOLATE FROSTING

Butter, 4 tablespoons
Chocolate, 1½ ounces
Salt, ⅛ teaspoon

Confectioners' sugar, 2 cups
Milk, 6 tablespoons
Vanilla, ½ teaspoon

Mix as bitter sweet chocolate frosting.
Yield: Enough for tops of two 9-inch layers.

## CREAMY CHOCOLATE FROSTING

Chocolate, 4 ounces
Condensed milk, 1 can
Water, 1 tablespoon

Melt the chocolate in the top of a double boiler. Add the condensed milk and cook over boiling water, stirring constantly, until it thickens (about 5 minutes). Add the water and blend it in well. Spread on a cool cake.
Yield: Enough for tops of two 9-inch layers.

## CHOCOLATE CREAM-CHEESE FROSTING

Cream cheese, 1 package
Milk, 2½ tablespoons

Confectioners' sugar, 2½ cups
Chocolate, 2 ounces
Salt, ⅛ teaspoon

Cream the cheese with the milk until fluffy. Add the sugar and cream the mixture well. Add the salt and the melted chocolate and blend thoroughly. Spread on cold cake.
Yield: Enough for tops of two 9-inch layers.

## MOCHA FROSTING

Butter, 5 tablespoons
Cocoa, 2 tablespoons

Confectioners' sugar, 2 cups
Strong coffee infusion,
    2 tablespoons
Salt, ⅛ teaspoon

Cream the butter and add the other ingredients. Cream together thoroughly and spread on a cold cake.
Yield: Enough for tops of two 9-inch layers.

## VANILLA FROSTING

Egg white, 1  
Salt, $\frac{1}{16}$ teaspoon  
Confectioners' sugar, 2 cups

Vanilla, $\frac{1}{2}$ teaspoon  
Milk, 2 tablespoons

Mix all ingredients, egg white unbeaten, and cream together well. Spread on a cool cake.

Yield: Enough for tops of two 9-inch layers.

## ORANGE FROSTING I

Egg yolk, 1  
Rind of 1 orange, grated  
Orange juice, 2 tablespoons

Lemon juice, 2 tablespoons  
Salt, $\frac{1}{8}$ teaspoon  
Confectioners' sugar, $2\frac{1}{2}$ cups

Mix all ingredients together thoroughly and spread on cake.

Yield: Enough for tops of two 9-inch layers.

## ORANGE FROSTING II

Rind of 1 orange, grated  
Orange juice, 2 tablespoons  
Lemon juice, 1 tablespoon

Confectioners' sugar, 3 cups  
Melted butter, 4 tablespoons

Mix the fruit juices and orange rind. Add one half the sugar and the melted butter and blend well. Add the remainder of the sugar and cream well. Spread on a cold cake.

Yield: Enough for tops and sides of two 9-inch layers.

## LEMON FROSTING

Egg, 1  
Rind of 1 lemon  
Confectioners' sugar, 3 cups

Lemon juice, 3 tablespoons  
Salt, $\frac{1}{8}$ teaspoon

Mix all ingredients (egg unbeaten) and cream well. Spread on a cool cake.

Yield: Enough for tops and sides of two 9-inch layers.

## JELLY FROSTING

This frosting is very light and delicate. It is best for sponge or angel cake but a filling of jelly and chopped nuts may be used between layers and this frosting used as a topping. If the jelly used is not tart enough lemon juice may be added.

**Currant or any tart jelly, ½ cup**
**Egg white, 1**
**Lemon juice, if desired**

Put the jelly and unbeaten egg white in the top of a double boiler over boiling water. Beat continuously with a rotary beater until it will hold up in peaks.

Yield: Enough for one angel food cake.

## MERINGUE TOPPING

(To be used in place of a frosting)

**Egg whites, 2**               **Sugar, 4 tablespoons**
**Vanilla, ½ teaspoon**         **Chopped nuts, ¼ cup**

Beat the egg whites until foamy. Add the vanilla and the sugar and continue beating until it holds up in peaks. Spread this meringue on top of any cake before baking and sprinkle it with the chopped nuts. Bake at the correct temperature for that particular cake. If layers are desired put them together with whipped cream and garnish the topping with whipped cream.

Yield: Enough for top of one 9-inch layer.

## CRUMB TOPPING

This gives an interesting finish to the top of any loaf cake. It may be sprinkled with chopped nuts or garnished with whole nuts if desired.

**Butter, ¼ cup**              **Flour, ½ cup**
**Sugar, ⅓ cup**              **Spice for flavoring, if desired**

Cream the butter. Add the sugar and cream well. Add the flour (and spice) and mix well and sprinkle like crumbs

over the unbaked loaf cake.  Bake at correct temperature for
that cake.

Yield: Enough for top of one loaf cake.

## ORNAMENTAL FROSTINGS

In decorating a cake with ornamental frosting two factors
are of great importance.  The first is the selection of the right
frosting, for not all kinds are suited to decorative purposes.
Butter frostings are easy to work with because they dry out
very slowly.  They keep better than the ones which contain
egg whites and therefore blend better with the cake.  Butter
frostings (see previous recipes) are not so good for fine detailed
work such as delicate stems and flowers.  For lacy work of this
kind use one of the recipes which follows.

The second important requirement for success in decorating cakes is to have a good frosting set.  They may be purchased in any household equipment shop, are not expensive
and, with the proper tubes, may be used for other purposes
such as meringues or hard sauce rosettes.

A cake which is to be decorated should be frosted very
smoothly.  If butter frosting is to be used for the ornamental
work it should also be used for frosting the cake.  If the cake
is to be decorated by using one of the frostings which contain
egg white it should be covered first with a smooth coating of
a cooked frosting.  The recipes for "Boiled Frosting I,"
"Boiled Frosting II" and "Quick Cooked Frosting" are excellent.  Allow the frosted cake to dry thoroughly before
applying the decorations.

A decorated cake may be pure white, as a bride's cake,
or it may be delicately tinted.  A Valentine's cake might be
white with pink trimmings and a Hallowe'en one frosted with
chocolate and trimmed with delicate orange colored frosting.

Before beginning to decorate the cake make a drawing of
the pattern to be used.  If you are an amateur, experiment
with the different details of your pattern before applying them
to the cake.  When practicing, work on a piece of waxed

paper and the frosting may then be scraped up and used again.  After you are satisfied with your results apply the design to the frosted cake.

## ORNAMENTAL FROSTING (UNCOOKED)

**Egg white, 1 unbeaten**
**Confectioners' sugar, sifted, 1½ cups**
**Cream of tartar, ¼ teaspoon**
*or*
**Lemon juice, 1 teaspoon**

Add ½ cup of the sugar to the egg white and beat until foamy.  Add the cream of tartar or lemon juice and another ½ cup of sugar and beat well.  Add the remainder of the sugar and beat until it holds up in sharp, thin peaks.  While working keep the extra frosting covered with a damp cloth and beat it up each time before filling the tube.

## ORNAMENTAL FROSTING (COOKED)

**Sugar, 2 cups**               **Water, ½ cup**
**Light corn syrup, ⅓ cup**     **Egg whites, 2**

Cook together the sugar, corn syrup and water to 242° F. (firm ball in cold water).  Remove from the fire and beat the egg whites until stiff but not dry.  Pour the syrup slowly into the egg whites, beating during the addition.  Continue beating until the mixture holds up in strong thin peaks.  Use immediately for decorating the cake.  Keep the bowl of extra frosting covered with a damp cloth.

## PETITS FOURS FROSTING

**Sugar, 2 cups**                    **Water, ¾ cup**
**Cream of tartar, ⅛ teaspoon**      **Confectioners' sugar**

Mix the sugar, cream of tartar and water and boil to 228° F. (a thin syrup).  Cool to lukewarm and add enough confectioners' sugar to make it the consistency of a soft frosting which can be poured.

To frost tiny cakes brush off all crumbs and arrange them close together, but not touching, in rows on a wire cooling rack. Pour the frosting in a steady stream over them so that the top and sides of each one is completely covered. Lift the rack and shake it gently to remove the frosting which clings to it. Scrape up the frosting which dripped through, re-heat it over hot water and use it again. If the first frosting was white, that which was re-heated might be delicately tinted in any desired color. Remove the cakes with a spatula and trim off excess frosting from the base of each. Decorate with candied fruits, nuts or ornamental frosting.

## Chapter 22:

# SYRUPS AND SAUCES

### CARAMEL SYRUP

Sugar, 1 cup
Boiling water, ½ cup or more

In a frying pan or a heavy aluminum saucepan heat the sugar over a very low flame, stirring constantly with a wooden spoon, until it is melted to a syrup. Remove from the flame and add the water slowly while stirring. Return to flame and allow it to simmer until it is a thin syrup. If there are any lumps add a little more water and boil it until the lumps have dissolved.

Caramel syrup may be used for waffles or griddle cakes either as it is or mixed with an equal amount of corn syrup. One-fourth teaspoon of vanilla may be added if desired. If it is to be used for this purpose the water must be added to the melted sugar when it is a very light golden brown. It is also used as a flavoring in candies, frostings, custards, ice cream and other desserts. If it is to be used as a flavoring material the sugar must be heated until it is a deep golden brown before adding the water in order to develop a strong caramel flavor.

When the boiling is finished the product must be a thin syrup. If not to be used immediately, keep it in a covered jar.

Yield: About ½ cup.

### CHOCOLATE SYRUP

Chocolate, 4 ounces          Water, ⅔ cup
Salt, ⅛ teaspoon             Sugar, 1 cup
            Vanilla, ¼ teaspoon, if desired

Melt the chocolate over hot water. Boil the sugar, salt and water. Add the melted chocolate and boil again, while stirring. Add vanilla.

Yield: About 1⅓ cups.

## COCOA SYRUP

| | |
|---|---|
| Cocoa, ½ cup | Salt, ⅛ teaspoon |
| Sugar, ⅔ cup | Water, 1 cup |

Vanilla, ¼ teaspoon, if desired

Mix cocoa, sugar, salt and water and boil, while stirring, for about two minutes. Add vanilla.

Yield: About 1¼ cups.

Either chocolate or cocoa syrup may be kept in a covered jar for several days in the refrigerator and used as needed. Both syrups may be used as the base for chocolate drinks. Two tablespoons of either syrup to one cup of milk will give a drink of proper strength for the average person. For a chocolate milk simply add the syrup to the milk and mix well.

This makes a good drink for children who are not fond of milk unless it is flavored.

## BROWN SUGAR SYRUP

| | |
|---|---|
| Light brown sugar, 1 cup | Water, ½ cup |
| Light corn syrup, ¼ cup | Salt, ¹⁄₁₆ teaspoon |

Vanilla, ¼ teaspoon

Mix the sugar, syrup, salt and water and cook, with occasional stirring, to 228° F. (a thin syrup). Cool and add vanilla. If a thermometer was not used and the syrup is too thick, add water to make it the desired consistency.

Yield: About ¾ cup.

## SAUCES

### FUDGE SAUCE

Sugar, 1 cup
Light corn syrup, 4 table-
spoons
Cocoa, 1/3 cup

Salt, 1/2 teaspoon
Water, 1/2 cup
Vanilla, 1 teaspoon
Butter, 2 tablespoons

Mix sugar, cocoa, salt, corn cyrup and water and cook to 228° F. (a thin syrup). Add butter and vanilla and mix. Do not beat. Serve warm or re-heat over water, with little stirring.
Yield: About 1 cup.

### CREAMY FUDGE SAUCE

Fudge sauce, 1/2 cup
Cream, 1/2 cup, whipped

Add the whipped cream to the fudge sauce and fold it in well.
Yield: About 1½ cups.

### BUTTERSCOTCH SAUCE

Brown sugar, 1¼ cups
Light corn syrup, 2/3 cup

Butter, 4 tablespoons
Vanilla, 1/2 teaspoon
Cream, 1/2 cup

Cook sugar, syrup and butter to 242° F. (firm ball in cold water), stirring until the sugar is dissolved. Add the vanilla and cream and cool before using.
Yield: About 1½ cups.

### GINGER SAUCE

Butterscotch sauce, 1 recipe
Preserved ginger, 1/4 to 1/2 cup

Chop the ginger finely and add it to the sauce.

## MINT DESSERT SAUCE

Mint jelly, ½ cup                 Water, ¼ cup
Marshmallows, 8              Egg white, 1
Lemon juice, to taste

Cut marshmallows into quarters and add to jelly and water in the top of a double boiler. Heat over water until marshmallows are melted. Mix well and pour over the stiffly beaten egg white, beating during the addition. Add one tablespoon of lemon juice, mix well, taste and add more if needed.

Yield: About 1½ cups.

## MARSHMALLOW SAUCE

Sugar, ⅔ cup                 Egg white, 1
Light corn syrup, 2 table-   Water, ½ cup
   spoons                    Marshmallows, 8

Cook the sugar, corn syrup and water to 236° F., stirring until the sugar is dissolved. Quarter the marshmallows and add them to the hot syrup. When softened add this mixture to the stiffly beaten egg white. Flavor with a few drops of vanilla or color green and flavor with mint.

Yield: About 2 cups.

## GINGER MARSHMALLOW SAUCE

Marshmallows, 16          Sugar, 4 tablespoons
Water, ⅓ cup               Preserved ginger, ¼ to ½ cup
Egg yolks, 3                Orange rind, ½ teaspoon
                           Lemon rind, ½ teaspoon

Steam marshmallows and water in the top of a double boiler until the marshmallows are melted. Beat egg yolks until light, add sugar and mix well and stir in the marshmallows. Add ginger, lemon and orange rind and return to the top of the double boiler. Cook two minutes longer. Cool before using.

## WHITE FOAMY SAUCE

Egg white, 1
Granulated sugar, 3 tablespoons

Vanilla, ½ teaspoon
Cream, ¼ cup

Beat the egg white until foamy.  Add the sugar and vanilla and continue beating until it holds up in peaks.  Whip the cream and fold it into the egg mixture.

Yield:  About 1¼ cups.

## FRUIT SAUCE

Canned fruit, 1 can
Lemon juice, 1 tablespoon

Using canned pineapple, apricots, peaches, etc., drain the juice from the fruit and boil it until it is reduced to half its original volume.  Add the sliced fruit and lemon juice and bring to the boiling point.  Cool before serving.

## YELLOW FOAMY SAUCE

Egg yolk, 1
Sugar, granulated or brown,
  2 tablespoons
Cream, ¼ cup

Egg white, 1
Sugar, granulated or brown,
  2 tablespoons
Vanilla, ½ teaspoon or grated
  rind of one orange or one
  lemon

Beat egg white until foamy.  Add 2 tablespoons of sugar and beat until stiff.  In another bowl beat the egg yolk well and add two tablespoons of sugar.  Whip the cream and add the flavoring.  Combine the two egg mixtures and fold in the whipped cream.

Yield:  About 1½ cups.

## ADA CUMMINS' RASPBERRY SAUCE

> Raspberries, fresh or frozen, 1 pint
> Sugar, 1 cup
> Lemon juice, 1 tablespoon

Crush the raspberries, add the sugar and lemon juice and allow the mixture to stand several hours before using.

## HARD SAUCE

| | |
|---|---|
| Butter, 1/3 cup | Liquid, 2 tablespoons |
| Sugar, confectioners' or light brown, 1 cup | Flavoring |
| | Salt, 1/8 teaspoon |

Cream the butter, add some of the sugar, then the remainder of the sugar and the liquid alternately, continuing the creaming until the mixture is fluffy and smooth.

If confectioners' sugar is used the flavoring may be 2/3 teaspoon vanilla. The liquid may be orange or lemon juice, in which case the grated rind of 1/2 orange should be added for flavor.

If brown sugar is used the liquid should be cream or milk and the flavoring vanilla.

For a mocha sauce use strong coffee for the liquid and 1 tablespoon cocoa and 1/2 teaspoon vanilla for additional flavoring. Either sugar may be used for mocha sauce.

Yield: About 2/3 cup.

# Chapter 23:

## REFRIGERATOR ICE CREAMS

Ever since the electric refrigerator has come into common use in the homes of the country efforts have been made to instruct the housewife regarding the making of frozen desserts. From the very beginning the manufacturers played up the ease with which America's favorite dessert—ice-cream—could be made at home. Some of the first results were very unsatisfactory. The most that could be said of them was that the desserts were cold and bore some resemblance to the products made by the old methods of freezing. Business and college laboratories began to experiment to overcome some of the difficulties and to see if they could find the right proportion of ingredients, and the right methods of combining and of handling them during the freezing process which would result in a grain as fine as that produced in the freezer where motion seemed a necessary part of the process.

After much investigation we believe that the following recipes will give perfect satisfaction, even to those whose standards for frozen desserts are very high.

General directions for all of the following ice cream recipes:

**Preparation of the refrigerator.**—About one hour before putting the mixture into the refrigerator set the temperature control at the coldest point possible. Keep it at this temperature until the ice cream is frozen; then, if desired, it may be raised slightly.

**Care during freezing.**—Pour the ice cream mixture into the refrigerator tray and beat it twice in the tray, with a rotary beater, during the freezing period. Beat it first after about 15 minutes when it is viscous and just beginning to freeze, and again in about half an hour when it is partially

163

frozen along the edges and bottom. The beating is easier if the tray is not too full. It is often wise to start the freezing using two trays and after the second beating to put all of the mixture into one tray for the final freezing. If the ice cream has been packed firmly it may be served in slices or dipped out with a spoon.

**Combining ingredients.**—There are three or four mixtures which are blended together in each recipe. The first is a custard, the second a meringue and the third whipped cream.

To make a custard scald the milk in the top of a double boiler. Beat the egg yolks, salt and sugar together until well blended, but not foamy. Add the scalded milk slowly while stirring constantly. Return the mixture to the double boiler and cook, with constant stirring, for about a minute or until the egg yolks are cooked sufficiently to give a coating to the spoon. The custard must be thoroughly cold when it is used.

The meringue is made of beaten egg whites and sugar. Beat the egg whites with a rotary beater until foamy. Add the sugar gradually and continue beating until the mixture will hold up in peaks. If the egg whites are beaten first the cream may be whipped without washing the beater.

Whip the cream until just barely stiff.

## VANILLA ICE CREAM I

**(1)**
Milk, 1 cup
Sugar, ⅓ cup
Flour, 1 tablespoon
Salt, ⅛ teaspoon
Egg yolks, 2

**(2)**
Egg whites, 2
Sugar, ⅓ cup
**(3)**
Heavy cream, 1¼ cups
Vanilla, 1½ teaspoons

Mix flour, sugar, and salt. Add milk and boil, while stirring, for about a minute. Cool slightly and stir into beaten egg yolks. Return to double boiler and continue as for custard. Chill well.

Make a meringue of materials in list 2 and add it to the cold custard.

Whip the cream, add it and vanilla to the custard-meringue mixture and beat together well with the rotary beater. Pour into refrigerator trays and freeze as directed.

## VANILLA ICE CREAM II

**(1)**
Gelatin, ½ teaspoon
Cold water, 1 tablespoon
**(2)**
Milk, 1 cup
Sugar, ⅓ cup
Salt, ⅛ teaspoon
Egg yolks, 2

**(3)**
Egg whites, 2
Sugar, ⅓ cup
**(4)**
Heavy cream, 1¼ cups
Vanilla, 1½ teaspoons

Soften the gelatin in the cold water. Add it to a hot custard made from the ingredients in list 2 and stir until thoroughly dissolved. Chill well. Make a meringue of materials in list 3 and combine the two mixtures. Whip the cream, add the vanilla and combine with the custard-meringue mixture. Pour into the refrigerator trays and freeze as directed.

## VANILLA ICE CREAM III

**(1)**
Evaporated milk, ⅓ cup
Milk, ⅔ cup
Sugar, ⅓ cup
Salt, ⅛ teaspoon
Egg yolks, 2

**(2)**
Egg whites, 2
Sugar, ⅓ cup
**(3)**
Heavy cream, 1¼ cups
Vanilla, 1½ teaspoons

Make a custard of materials in list 1 and cool it thoroughly. Make a meringue of ingredients in list 2 and combine the two mixtures. Whip the cream, add the vanilla and add it to the custard-meringue mixture. Beat together well and pour into the refrigerator trays. Freeze as directed.

## CHOCOLATE ICE CREAM

**(1)**
Evaporated milk, ⅓ cup
Milk, ⅔ cup
Sugar, ⅓ cup
Salt, ⅛ teaspoon
Egg yolks, 2
Unsweetened chocolate,
    1½ ounces

**(2)**
Egg whites, 2
Sugar, ⅓ cup
**(3)**
Heavy cream, 1¼ cups
Vanilla, 1 teaspoon

Melt the chocolate in the top of a double boiler and stir into it about half of the sugar. Blend well and add the evaporated milk slowly, while stirring, so as to keep the mixture smooth. Add the fresh milk, blend it in well and with this mixture make a custard, using the rest of the sugar, the salt and the egg yolks. Chill well. Make a meringue of the materials in list 2 and add it to the cold chocolate custard. Whip the cream, add the vanilla and combine with the custard-meringue mixture, mixing them together well. Pour into refrigerator trays and freeze as directed.

## CARAMEL ICE CREAM

**(1)**
Milk, ⅔ cup
Heavy dark caramel syrup,
    ⅓ cup
Egg yolks, 2
Salt, ⅛ teaspoon

**(2)**
Egg whites, 2
Sugar, 2 tablespoons
**(3)**
Heavy cream, 1¼ cups
Vanilla, ½ teaspoon

Make the caramel syrup according to directions on page 157. Scald the milk and add the caramel syrup to it. Make a custard of this mixture and the egg yolks and salt. Cool thoroughly. Make a meringue of the ingredients in list 2 and add it to the cold caramel custard. Whip the cream, add the vanilla and combine with the custard-meringue mixture. Pour into the refrigerator trays and freeze as directed.

## COFFEE ICE CREAM

**(1)**
Evaporated milk, ½ cup
Strong coffee, ½ cup
Sugar, ⅓ cup
Salt, ⅛ teaspoon
Egg yolks, 2

**(2)**
Egg whites, 2
Sugar, ⅓ cup
**(3)**
Heavy cream, 1¼ cups
Vanilla, 1 teaspoon

Make strong coffee by using 4 tablespoons coffee to 1 cup of water. Combine coffee and evaporated milk and heat in a double boiler. Use it with the rest of the materials in list 1 for making a custard. Chill thoroughly. Make a meringue of the ingredients in list 2 and add it to the cold coffee custard. Whip the cream, add the vanilla and combine well with the custard-meringue mixture. Pour into the refrigerator trays and freeze as directed.

## STRAWBERRY ICE CREAM

**(1)**
Milk, 1 cup
Sugar, ⅓ cup
Flour, 1½ tablespoons
Salt, ⅛ teaspoon
Egg yolks, 2

**(2)**
Egg whites, 2
Sugar, ⅓ cup
**(3)**
Strawberries, 1 quart
Juice of 1 lemon
Sugar, ¾ cup
Heavy cream, 1¼ cups

Make a custard of materials in list 1 and chill it well. Make a meringue of ingredients in list 2 and add it to the cold custard. Crush the strawberries, strain if desired, and add sugar and lemon juice. Whip the cream and add it and the strawberry mixture to the custard-meringue mixture. Blend together well and pour into the refrigerator trays. Freeze as directed.

## TERMS IN GENERAL USE TO DESCRIBE OVEN TEMPERATURES USED IN THE RECIPES WHICH FOLLOW

| TERMS | TEMPERATURES |
|---|---|
| Slow | 250° F. to 350° F. |
| Moderate | 350° F. to 400° F. |
| Hot | 400° F. to 450° F. |

## ALMOND MACAROONS

> Almond paste, ¾ cup
> Egg whites, 2
> Powdered sugar, 1½ cups

Knead the almond paste with half the sugar. Add the egg whites one at a time and work each in well. Add remainder of sugar and knead thoroughly. Drop on a tin covered with greased paper and bake at 370° F. for about 15 minutes.

If the paper sticks, invert it with the cookies and steam it loose with a damp towel.

Yield: About 18 macaroons.

## COCOANUT MACAROONS

Condensed milk, ½ cup          Shredded cocoanut, 2 cups
Salt, ⅛ teaspoon               Vanilla, ½ teaspoon

Mix all ingredients together and drop from a teaspoon on a well greased baking sheet one inch apart. Bake at 350° F. until a delicate brown.

Yield: About 24 macaroons.

## SEA FOAM MACAROONS

Egg white, 1
Salt, 1/8 teaspoon

Brown sugar, 1 cup
Flour, 2 tablespoons
Chopped nuts, 1 cup

Beat the egg white until stiff. Mix salt, flour and sugar and fold into the egg white. Mix in chopped nuts. Drop from a teaspoon on a greased baking sheet and bake at 325° F. for 15 minutes. Cool slightly before removing from pan.

Yield: About 24 macaroons.

## CORNFLAKE MACAROONS

Egg whites, 3
Salt, 1/8 teaspoon
Sugar, 2/3 cup

Cornflakes or other dry
cereal, 2 1/2 cups
Vanilla, 1/2 teaspoon
Nuts or cocoanut, 1 cup

Add salt to egg whites and beat until stiff. Add vanilla and sugar, gradually, and beat until it holds up in peaks. Fold in cornflakes and nuts. Drop from a teaspoon on a greased baking sheet and bake at 325° F. for 15 minutes.

Yield: About 24 macaroons.

## COCOANUT CREAM BISCUITS

| LARGE RECIPE | SMALL RECIPE |
|---|---|
| Fresh cocoanut, grated, 4 cups | Fresh cocoanut, grated, 2 cups |
| Sugar, 1 cup | Sugar, 1/2 cup |
| Light corn syrup, 3/8 cup | Light corn syrup, 3 table-spoons |
| Water, 1 1/2 cups | Water, 1 cup |

This recipe contains a large proportion of cocoanut with only enough syrup to hold it together, hence it must be watched carefully while cooking.

Put all of the ingredients into a saucepan and cook, stirring to prevent burning to 240° F. (soft ball in cold water). At this temperature the mixture may become delicate brown in color.

Remove from fire and pour out on a greased slab or a greased, inverted pan or baking sheet. Roll with a rolling pin until about one-half inch thick. Cut with a small biscuit cutter.

Place on a greased, inverted baking sheet or pan and bake in a hot oven just long enough to brown the top. If the biscuits do not brown quickly, place under the broiler for a minute to brown the top. If the biscuits are baked too long, they become hard and brittle; they should be soft on the inside.

Yield (large recipe): twenty-four biscuits.

## COCOANUT BISCUITS

> Desiccated cocoanut, chopped, 2 cups
> Light corn syrup, ¼ cup
> Sugar, ¼ cup
> Flour, ¼ cup
> Egg white, 1

Put cocoanut through the food chopper. Coarse cocoanut spoils the shape of the biscuits.

Beat the egg white until stiff. Gradually fold in the sugar, flour, corn syrup, and cocoanut. Drop on a greased baking sheet. Form biscuits with the hands, making them flat on top and regular in shape.

Bake at 410° F. for ten minutes. If at the end of this time they are not brown, slip them under the broiler just long enough to color them. Too long baking makes biscuits dry and hard. They should be soft inside.

Yield: twelve biscuits.

## POP CORN LACE

| LARGE RECIPE | SMALL RECIPE |
|---|---|
| Butter, 2 tablespoons | Butter, 1 tablespoon |
| Sugar, 1 cup | Sugar, ½ cup |
| Popped corn, chopped, 2 cups | Popped corn, chopped, 1 cup |
| Baking powder, ¼ teaspoon | Baking powder, ⅛ teaspoon |
| Salt, ½ teaspoon | Salt, ¼ teaspoon |
| Eggs, 2 | Egg, 1 |

Cream the butter.  Add the sugar, well mixed with the baking powder and salt.  Cream together.  Add beaten egg and mix thoroughly.  Add chopped, popped corn and stir well.

Drop by teaspoonfuls on greased baking sheet or inverted pan.  As these cookies will spread in baking only a level teaspoonful should be allowed for each cookie and they should not be placed too close together.  Flatten with a spatula before placing in the oven.

Bake at 350° F. for about ten minutes.  When done the cookies should be delicately brown and very thin and lace-like.  Remove from baking sheet while still warm, because these cookies become very brittle when cold.  If they become too crisp, the cookies may be returned to the oven to heat until they soften.

Yield (large recipe): fifty small cookies.

## CORNLETS

| LARGE RECIPE | SMALL RECIPE |
|---|---|
| Popped corn, chopped, 4 cups | Popped corn, chopped, 2 cups |
| Egg whites, 2 | Egg white, 1 |
| Light corn syrup, ½ cup | Light corn syrup, ¼ cup |
| Brown sugar, ½ cup | Brown sugar, ¼ cup |
| Flour, ½ cup | Flour, ¼ cup |
| Almonds, blanched and chopped, ¼ cup | Almonds, blanched and chopped, 2 tablespoons |

Beat the egg whites until stiff. Gradually fold in the sugar, syrup, flour, and chopped, popped corn.

Drop on a slightly buttered baking sheet or inverted pan, forming biscuits about one and three-fourths inches in diameter. Sprinkle the tops of the biscuits with chopped, blanched almonds.

Bake at 350° F. for fifteen minutes.

Remove from baking sheet while still warm, because these cookies become very brittle when cold.

Yield (large recipe): thirty biscuits.

**Dusky Maidens.**—Make cornlets following directions given above. Do not sprinkle the tops of the cookies with almonds, as a smooth surface is desired. When the cookies have been removed from the pan and have become cool, draw faces on them with melted chocolate, using a tooth pick or a small brush.

A great deal of ingenuity can be exercised in the drawing of these faces, and the decorated cookies are appropriate for children's parties.

## BAKED FUDGE

| LARGE RECIPE | SMALL RECIPE |
|---|---|
| Eggs, 2 | Egg, 1 |
| Sugar, 1 cup | Sugar, ½ cup |
| Flour, ½ cup | Flour, ¼ cup |
| Butter, ⅓ cup | Butter, 2½ tablespoons |
| Chocolate, 4 squares | Chocolate, 2 squares |
| (4 ounces) | (2 ounces) |
| Nut meats, ½ cup | Nut meats, ¼ cup |
| Vanilla, 1 teaspoon | Vanilla, ½ teaspoon |
| Salt, ¼ teaspoon | Salt, ⅛ teaspoon |

Melt chocolate and butter. Beat eggs with sugar and add to chocolate mixture. Add other ingredients. Fill buttered pan to ⅓ inch and bake at 350° F. for about 25 minutes. When cool, cut into squares.

Yield (large recipe): sixteen squares.

## BAKED NUT SQUARES

| LARGE RECIPE | SMALL RECIPE |
|---|---|
| Eggs, 3 | Eggs, 2 |
| Brown sugar, 1½ cups | Brown sugar, 1 cup |
| Flour, ¾ cup | Flour, ½ cup |
| Baking powder, ¾ teaspoon | Baking powder, ½ teaspoon |
| Nut meats, 1 cup | Nut meats, ⅔ cup |
| Dates, ½ cup | Dates, ⅓ cup |

Break the nut meats into small pieces and freshen them in the oven. Wash the dates, dry them, remove the seeds, and cut them into small pieces.

Beat the eggs until light; add sugar and beat until thoroughly blended. Add the flour and baking powder which have been sifted together; mix well; add nuts and dates and stir through the dough.

Spread the mixture in a layer one-half inch thick in greased, shallow pans. Bake at 350° F. for twenty minutes, or until the mixture is firm.

Remove from the pan, and while warm cut into small squares or rectangles. Cover with powdered sugar, if desired.

Yield (large recipe): eighty small squares.

## FRUIT CAKE

| | |
|---|---|
| Butter, 1 pound | Soda, 1 teaspoon |
| Light brown sugar, 1 pound | Grape juice, 1 cup |
| Eggs, 9 | Currants, 3 pounds |
| Flour, 1 pound | Seeded raisins, 2 pounds |
| Mace, 1 teaspoon | Candied cherries, ½ pound |
| Cinnamon, 2 teaspoons | Candied pineapple, 1 pound |
| | Citron, 1 pound |

Cut raisins and cherries in half, slice pineapple and citron very thinly, wash currants well and dry them. Add one cup of the flour to the fruit and mix together well, coating them thoroughly.

Sift remaining flour with the other dry ingredients. Cream the butter and sugar, add the beaten egg yolks, part of the dry ingredients and then the grape juice and dry ingredients alternately. Fold in the beaten egg whites and mix batter and fruit thoroughly.

Line pans with two or three thicknesses of paper, allowing paper to extend over edge about 1/2 inch. Grease paper and fill pans 3/4 full. Cover with a piece of greased paper and a piece of cheese cloth and tie on securely and steam. A small cake will require about four hours. It may then be dried out in the oven at 250° F. for about 30 minutes. Fruit cake may be baked instead of steamed. A small one requires about 2 1/2 hours at 250° F.

Yield: weight—about 11 pounds.

## FRUIT CAKE SUPREME

| | |
|---|---|
| Raisins, 6 pounds | Brown sugar, 1 pound |
| Currants, 3 pounds | Butter, 1 pound |
| Citron, 2 pounds | Eggs, 12 |
| Candied cherries, 2 pounds | Baking powder, 1 teaspoon |
| Candied apricots, 2 pounds | Cinnamon, 2 teaspoons |
| Candied pineapple, 2 pounds | Cloves, 1 teaspoon |
| Flour, 4 cups | Nutmeg, 2 tablespoons |
| | Strong coffee, 1 cup |

Cut raisins and cherries in half. Slice citron, apricots and pineapple thinly. Wash currants well and dry them. Add one half of the flour to the fruit and mix well, coating the fruit thoroughly.

Sift remaining flour with the other dry ingredients. Cream the butter and sugar, add the beaten egg yolks, part of the dry ingredients and then the coffee and remaining dry ingredients alternately. Fold in the beaten egg whites and mix batter and fruit well.

Line pans with two or three thicknesses of paper, allowing paper to extend over edges about 1/2 inch. Grease paper and fill pans ¾ full. Cover with a greased paper and a piece of cheese cloth and tie them on securely and steam the cake. A small cake will require four hours. It may then be dried out in the oven at 250° F. for about 30 minutes. Fruit cake may be baked instead of steamed. A small one requires about 2½ hours at 250° F.

Yield: weight—about 21 pounds.

## CHOCOLATE CONFECTION DE LUXE

**Bitter chocolate, 4 ounces**
**Condensed milk, 1 can**
**Vanilla, 1 teaspoon**
**Fine vanilla wafer crumbs, 2 cups**
**Chopped nuts, 1 cup**
**Confectioners' sugar**

Put chocolate in the top of a double boiler, over hot water. When melted stir in condensed milk and cook until it is the consistency of a custard. Add the vanilla and fold in the vanilla wafer crumbs and the nuts. Blend thoroughly.

Spread the mixture to the thickness of one-half inch in a pan and allow it to stand in the refrigerator until firm. Cut in squares and roll in confectioners' sugar. Wrap each piece in waxed paper and keep in a tin in the refrigerator.

Yield: about thirty squares.

# Chapter 25:
## SUGGESTIONS FOR SEQUENCE IN THE TEACHING OF CANDY MAKING

In teaching candy making it is desirable to have each student make candy by herself in order that she may have practice in making the cold water tests and reading her own thermometer.

The large recipes given are about the size which would usually be made at home. The smaller ones are suitable for use in teaching, both from the standpoint of equipment and of amount of material to be used, but are large enough to give experience in handling the candy.

The processes involving unusual manipulation were demonstrated before the class.

In planning our sequence of lessons we began with the types of candy that would not be spoiled by having the temperature a few degrees higher or lower than that called for in the recipe. At first it is difficult for the student to read the thermometer accurately and quickly or to judge the cold water test.

Butterscotch and peanut brittle are good types of candy for a first lesson because they require little manipulation. Taffy was included in our first lesson because we were teaching college students, most of whom had had some experience in taffy pulling. With a large class of children, a taffy lesson, where every one pulls taffy at once, is quite an undertaking. It would be simpler to let the class become experienced in the ways of candy pulling a few at a time.

Fondant was taught in our second lesson because this is the simplest of the cream candies. A fondant failure can be recooked easily and the time of cooking is short.

We gave time during two lessons to caramels and nougat

so that the candy could be made in one lesson and cut and wrapped in the next.   Both of these candies require long cooking and can scarcely be made and wrapped in one period.

In each lesson special attention was given to the appearance of the finished candy.   The students realized the importance of cutting the candy in uniform pieces of the proper size. When wrapping was done the candy was made to look as professional as possible.

One lesson was devoted to box packing and the accessories which make candy boxes attractive.

Our aim was to teach in a short intensive course, the making of candies for home and school—not to train commercial candy makers.

The following outline may prove suggestive and selections can be made from it to suit the time available for candy making in any cookery course.   A three-hour period was given to each lesson.

## LESSON 1—TAFFIES AND BRITTLES

Demonstration—pulled mints to show taffy pulling.
Class work—each student made either taffy or brittle, choosing
    from a variety of recipes, such as sea side taffy, cream
    taffy, honey taffy, chocolate taffy, etc., to show the range
    of possibilities.

## LESSON 2—FONDANT AND POP CORN

Demonstration—the paddling and kneading of fondant.
Class work—each student made fondant, different recipes being
    chosen.
Pop corn balls and bricks were made to review the principles
    of taffies and brittles.   Two students worked together on
    a pop corn recipe.

### LESSON 3—FUDGE, PENUCHI, OPERAS, MAPLE CAN-DIES AND SIMILAR CREAM CANDIES, DIVINITY

Demonstration—divinity.

Class work—each student made fudge or a similar cream candy.

Two students working together made divinity.

### LESSON 4—CARAMELS

Demonstration—the dipping of caramel nut rolls.

Class work—each student made caramels, different recipes being chosen.  The nuts were prepared for the nougat to be made in the following lesson.

### LESSON 5—NOUGAT

Demonstration—the cutting and wrapping of caramels.

Class work—each student made nougat and wrapped her cara-mels made the previous lesson.  The making of nougat does not need to be demonstrated since the general prin-ciples are those of divinity.

### LESSON 6—COCOANUT CANDIES, NUTS, RAISINS, AND ACCESSORIES

Demonstration—chocolate coating and spiced nuts.

Class work—each student wrapped nougat made the previous lesson, prepared spiced raisins and cocoanut candy, and practiced chocolate dipping.

### LESSON 7—SUPER FUDGE, MOLDING, AND REVIEW

Demonstration—the molding of candies from super fudge, as fudge marbles, double deckers, etc.

Class work—each student made one review recipe.  Two stu-dents working together made super fudge and molded it.

## LESSON 8—PACKING THE BOX

Demonstration—the packing of a box of candy.

Class work—each student prepared accessories, such as stuffed cherries, prunes, raisins, and dates, and used them in packing boxes of candy.

Candies for the boxes had been kept from previous lessons.

# Index

**181**

# A CATALOGUE OF SELECTED DOVER BOOKS
## IN ALL FIELDS OF INTEREST

# A CATALOGUE OF SELECTED DOVER BOOKS IN ALL FIELDS OF INTEREST

CELESTIAL OBJECTS FOR COMMON TELESCOPES, T. W. Webb. The most used book in amateur astronomy: inestimable aid for locating and identifying nearly 4,000 celestial objects. Edited, updated by Margaret W. Mayall. 77 illustrations. Total of 645pp. 5⅜ x 8½.
20917-2, 20918-0 Pa., Two-vol. set $9.00

HISTORICAL STUDIES IN THE LANGUAGE OF CHEMISTRY, M. P. Crosland. The important part language has played in the development of chemistry from the symbolism of alchemy to the adoption of systematic nomenclature in 1892. ". . . wholeheartedly recommended,"—Science. 15 illustrations. 416pp. of text. 5⅝ x 8¼. 63702-6 Pa. $6.00

BURNHAM'S CELESTIAL HANDBOOK, Robert Burnham, Jr. Thorough, readable guide to the stars beyond our solar system. Exhaustive treatment, fully illustrated. Breakdown is alphabetical by constellation: Andromeda to Cetus in Vol. 1; Chamaeleon to Orion in Vol. 2; and Pavo to Vulpecula in Vol. 3. Hundreds of illustrations. Total of about 2000pp. 6⅛ x 9¼.
23567-X, 23568-8, 23673-0 Pa., Three-vol. set $27.85

THEORY OF WING SECTIONS: INCLUDING A SUMMARY OF AIRFOIL DATA, Ira H. Abbott and A. E. von Doenhoff. Concise compilation of subatomic aerodynamic characteristics of modern NASA wing sections, plus description of theory. 350pp. of tables. 693pp. 5⅜ x 8½.
60586-8 Pa. $8.50

DE RE METALLICA, Georgius Agricola. Translated by Herbert C. Hoover and Lou H. Hoover. The famous Hoover translation of greatest treatise on technological chemistry, engineering, geology, mining of early modern times (1556). All 289 original woodcuts. 638pp. 6¾ x 11.
60006-8 Clothbd. $17.95

THE ORIGIN OF CONTINENTS AND OCEANS, Alfred Wegener. One of the most influential, most controversial books in science, the classic statement for continental drift. Full 1966 translation of Wegener's final (1929) version. 64 illustrations. 246pp. 5⅜ x 8½. 61708-4 Pa. $4.50

THE PRINCIPLES OF PSYCHOLOGY, William James. Famous long course complete, unabridged. Stream of thought, time perception, memory, experimental methods; great work decades ahead of its time. Still valid, useful; read in many classes. 94 figures. Total of 1391pp. 5⅜ x 8½.
20381-6, 20382-4 Pa., Two-vol. set $13.00

THE COMPLETE BOOK OF DOLL MAKING AND COLLECTING, Catherine Christopher. Instructions, patterns for dozens of dolls, from rag doll on up to elaborate, historically accurate figures. Mould faces, sew clothing, make doll houses, etc. Also collecting information. Many illustrations. 288pp. 6 x 9. 22066-4 Pa. $4.50

THE DAGUERREOTYPE IN AMERICA, Beaumont Newhall. Wonderful portraits, 1850's townscapes, landscapes; full text plus 104 photographs. The basic book. Enlarged 1976 edition. 272pp. 8¼ x 11¼.
23322-7 Pa. $7.95

CRAFTSMAN HOMES, Gustav Stickley. 296 architectural drawings, floor plans, and photographs illustrate 40 different kinds of "Mission-style" homes from *The Craftsman* (1901-16), voice of American style of simplicity and organic harmony. Thorough coverage of Craftsman idea in text and picture, now collector's item. 224pp. 8⅛ x 11. 23791-5 Pa. $6.00

PEWTER-WORKING: INSTRUCTIONS AND PROJECTS, Burl N. Osborn. & Gordon O. Wilber. Introduction to pewter-working for amateur craftsman. History and characteristics of pewter; tools, materials, step-by-step instructions. Photos, line drawings, diagrams. Total of 160pp. 7⅞ x 10¾. 23786-9 Pa. $3.50

THE GREAT CHICAGO FIRE, edited by David Lowe. 10 dramatic, eyewitness accounts of the 1871 disaster, including one of the aftermath and rebuilding, plus 70 contemporary photographs and illustrations of the ruins—courthouse, Palmer House, Great Central Depot, etc. Introduction by David Lowe. 87pp. 8¼ x 11. 23771-0 Pa. $4.00

SILHOUETTES: A PICTORIAL ARCHIVE OF VARIED ILLUSTRATIONS, edited by Carol Belanger Grafton. Over 600 silhouettes from the 18th to 20th centuries include profiles and full figures of men and women, children, birds and animals, groups and scenes, nature, ships, an alphabet. Dozens of uses for commercial artists and craftspeople. 144pp. 8⅜ x 11¼.
23781-8 Pa. $4.50

ANIMALS: 1,419 COPYRIGHT-FREE ILLUSTRATIONS OF MAMMALS, BIRDS, FISH, INSECTS, ETC., edited by Jim Harter. Clear wood engravings present, in extremely lifelike poses, over 1,000 species of animals. One of the most extensive copyright-free pictorial sourcebooks of its kind. Captions. Index. 284pp. 9 x 12. 23766-4 Pa. $8.95

INDIAN DESIGNS FROM ANCIENT ECUADOR, Frederick W. Shaffer. 282 original designs by pre-Columbian Indians of Ecuador (500-1500 A.D.). Designs include people, mammals, birds, reptiles, fish, plants, heads, geometric designs. Use as is or alter for advertising, textiles, leathercraft, etc. Introduction. 95pp. 8¾ x 11¼. 23764-8 Pa. $3.50

SZIGETI ON THE VIOLIN, Joseph Szigeti. Genial, loosely structured tour by premier violinist, featuring a pleasant mixture of reminiscenes, insights into great music and musicians, innumerable tips for practicing violinists. 385 musical passages. 256pp. 5⅝ x 8¼. 23763-X Pa. $4.00

TONE POEMS, SERIES II: TILL EULENSPIEGELS LUSTIGE STREICHE, ALSO SPRACH ZARATHUSTRA, AND EIN HELDEN-LEBEN, Richard Strauss. Three important orchestral works, including very popular *Till Eulenspiegel's Marry Pranks,* reproduced in full score from original editions. Study score. 315pp. 9⅜ x 12¼. (Available in U.S. only)
23755-9 Pa. $8.95

TONE POEMS, SERIES I: DON JUAN, TOD UND VERKLARUNG AND DON QUIXOTE, Richard Strauss. Three of the most often performed and recorded works in entire orchestral repertoire, reproduced in full score from original editions. Study score. 286pp. 9⅜ x 12¼. (Available in U.S. only)
23754-0 Pa. $7.50

11 LATE STRING QUARTETS, Franz Joseph Haydn. The form which Haydn defined and "brought to perfection." (*Grove's*). 11 string quartets in complete score, his last and his best. The first in a projected series of the complete Haydn string quartets. Reliable modern Eulenberg edition, otherwise difficult to obtain. 320pp. 8⅜ x 11¼. (Available in U.S. only)
23753-2 Pa. $7.50

FOURTH, FIFTH AND SIXTH SYMPHONIES IN FULL SCORE, Peter Ilyitch Tchaikovsky. Complete orchestral scores of Symphony No. 4 in F Minor, Op. 36; Symphony No. 5 in E Minor, Op. 64; Symphony No. 6 in B Minor, "Pathetique," Op. 74. Bretikopf & Hartel eds. Study score. 480pp. 9⅜ x 12¼.
23861-X Pa. $10.95

THE MARRIAGE OF FIGARO: COMPLETE SCORE, Wolfgang A. Mozart. Finest comic opera ever written. Full score, not to be confused with piano renderings. Peters edition. Study score. 448pp. 9⅜ x 12¼. (Available in U.S. only)
23751-6 Pa. $11.95

"IMAGE" ON THE ART AND EVOLUTION OF THE FILM, edited by Marshall Deutelbaum. Pioneering book brings together for first time 38 groundbreaking articles on early silent films from *Image* and 263 illustrations newly shot from rare prints in the collection of the International Museum of Photography. A landmark work. Index. 256pp. 8¼ x 11.
23777-X Pa. $8.95

AROUND-THE-WORLD COOKY BOOK, Lois Lintner Sumption and Marguerite Lintner Ashbrook. 373 cooky and frosting recipes from 28 countries (America, Austria, China, Russia, Italy, etc.) include Viennese kisses, rice wafers, London strips, lady fingers, hony, sugar spice, maple cookies, etc. Clear instructions. All tested. 38 drawings. 182pp. 5⅜ x 8.
23802-4 Pa. $2.50

THE ART NOUVEAU STYLE, edited by Roberta Waddell. 579 rare photographs, not available elsewhere, of works in jewelry, metalwork, glass, ceramics, textiles, architecture and furniture by 175 artists—Mucha, Seguy, Lalique, Tiffany, Gaudin, Hohlwein, Saarinen, and many others. 288pp. 8⅜ x 11¼.
23515-7 Pa. $6.95

THE AMERICAN SENATOR, Anthony Trollope. Little known, long un-available Trollope novel on a grand scale. Here are humorous comment on American vs. English culture, and stunning portrayal of a heroine/villainess. Superb evocation of Victorian village life. 561pp. 5⅜ x 8½.
23801-6 Pa. $6.00

WAS IT MURDER? James Hilton. The author of *Lost Horizon* and *Good-bye, Mr. Chips* wrote one detective novel (under a pen-name) which was quickly forgotten and virtually lost, even at the height of Hilton's fame. This edition brings it back—a finely crafted public school puzzle resplendent with Hilton's stylish atmosphere. A thoroughly English thriller by the creator of Shangri-la. 252pp. 5⅜ x 8. (Available in U.S. only)
23774-5 Pa. $3.00

CENTRAL PARK: A PHOTOGRAPHIC GUIDE, Victor Laredo and Henry Hope Reed. 121 superb photographs show dramatic views of Central Park: Bethesda Fountain, Cleopatra's Needle, Sheep Meadow, the Blockhouse, plus people engaged in many park activities: ice skating, bike riding, etc. Captions by former Curator of Central Park, Henry Hope Reed, provide historical view, changes, etc. Also photos of N.Y. landmarks on park's periphery. 96pp. 8½ x 11.
23750-8 Pa. $4.50

NANTUCKET IN THE NINETEENTH CENTURY, Clay Lancaster. 180 rare photographs, stereographs, maps, drawings and floor plans recreate unique American island society. Authentic scenes of shipwreck, light-houses, streets, homes are arranged in geographic sequence to provide walking-tour guide to old Nantucket existing today. Introduction, captions. 160pp. 8⅞ x 11¾.
23747-8 Pa. $6.95

STONE AND MAN: A PHOTOGRAPHIC EXPLORATION, Andreas Feininger. 106 photographs by *Life* photographer Feininger portray man's deep passion for stone through the ages. Stonehenge-like megaliths, forti-fied towns, sculpted marble and crumbling tenements show textures, beau-ties, fascination. 128pp. 9¼ x 10¾.
23756-7 Pa. $5.95

CIRCLES, A MATHEMATICAL VIEW, D. Pedoe. Fundamental aspects of college geometry, non-Euclidean geometry, and other branches of mathe-matics: representing circle by point. Poincare model, isoperimetric prop-erty, etc. Stimulating recreational reading. 66 figures. 96pp. 5⅝ x 8¼.
63698-4 Pa. $2.75

THE DISCOVERY OF NEPTUNE, Morton Grosser. Dramatic scientific history of the investigations leading up to the actual discovery of the eighth planet of our solar system. Lucid, well-researched book by well-known historian of science. 172pp. 5⅜ x 8½.
23726-5 Pa. $3.50

THE DEVIL'S DICTIONARY. Ambrose Bierce. Barbed, bitter, brilliant witticisms in the form of a dictionary. Best, most ferocious satire America has produced. 145pp. 5⅜ x 8½.
20487-1 Pa. $2.25

THE CURVES OF LIFE, Theodore A. Cook. Examination of shells, leaves, horns, human body, art, etc., in "*the* classic reference on how the golden ratio applies to spirals and helices in nature . . . ."—Martin Gardner. 426 illustrations. Total of 512pp. 5⅜ x 8½.                     23701-X Pa. $5.95

AN ILLUSTRATED FLORA OF THE NORTHERN UNITED STATES AND CANADA, Nathaniel L. Britton, Addison Brown. Encyclopedic work covers 4666 species, ferns on up. Everything. Full botanical information, illustration for each. This earlier edition is preferred by many to more recent revisions. 1913 edition. Over 4000 illustrations, total of 2087pp. 6⅛ x 9¼.                     22642-5, 22643-3, 22644-1 Pa., Three-vol. set $25.50

MANUAL OF THE GRASSES OF THE UNITED STATES, A. S. Hitchcock, U.S. Dept. of Agriculture. The basic study of American grasses, both indigenous and escapes, cultivated and wild. Over 1400 species. Full descriptions, information. Over 1100 maps, illustrations. Total of 1051pp. 5⅜ x 8½..                     22717-0, 22718-9 Pa., Two-vol. set $15.00

THE CACTACEAE,, Nathaniel L. Britton, John N. Rose. Exhaustive, definitive. Every cactus in the world. Full botanical descriptions. Thorough statement of nomenclatures, habitat, detailed finding keys. The one book needed by every cactus enthusiast. Over 1275 illustrations. Total of 1080pp. 8 x 10¼.                     21191-6, 21192-4 Clothbd., Two-vol. set $35.00

AMERICAN MEDICINAL PLANTS, Charles F. Millspaugh. Full descriptions, 180 plants covered: history; physical description; methods of preparation with all chemical constituents extracted; all claimed curative or adverse effects. 180 full-page plates. Classification table. 804pp. 6½ x 9¼.
                                        23034-1 Pa. $12.95

A MODERN HERBAL, Margaret Grieve. Much the fullest, most exact, most useful compilation of herbal material. Gigantic alphabetical encyclopedia, from aconite to zedoary, gives botanical information, medical properties, folklore, economic uses, and much else. Indispensable to serious reader. 161 illustrations. 888pp. 6½ x 9¼. (Available in U.S. only)
                                        22798-7, 22799-5 Pa., Two-vol. set $13.00

THE HERBAL or GENERAL HISTORY OF PLANTS, John Gerard. The 1633 edition revised and enlarged by Thomas Johnson. Containing almost 2850 plant descriptions and 2705 superb illustrations, Gerard's *Herbal* is a monumental work, the book all modern English herbals are derived from, the one herbal every serious enthusiast should have in its entirety. Original editions are worth perhaps $750. 1678pp. 8½ x 12¼.
                                        23147-X Clothbd. $50.00

MANUAL OF THE TREES OF NORTH AMERICA, Charles S. Sargent. The basic survey of every native tree and tree-like shrub, 717 species in all. Extremely full descriptions, information on habitat, growth, locales, economics, etc. Necessary to every serious tree lover. Over 100 finding keys. 783 illustrations. Total of 986pp. 5⅜ x 8½.
                                        20277-1, 20278-X Pa., Two-vol. set $11.00

AMERICAN BIRD ENGRAVINGS, Alexander Wilson et al. All 76 plates. from Wilson's *American Ornithology* (1808-14), most important ornithological work before Audubon, plus 27 plates from the supplement (1825-33) by Charles Bonaparte. Over 250 birds portrayed. 8 plates also reproduced in full color. 111pp. 9⅜ x 12½.                    23195-X Pa. $6.00

CRUICKSHANK'S PHOTOGRAPHS OF BIRDS OF AMERICA, Allan D. Cruickshank. Great ornithologist, photographer presents 177 closeups, groupings, panoramas, flightings, etc., of about 150 different birds. Expanded *Wings in the Wilderness*. Introduction by Helen G. Cruickshank. 191pp. 8¼ x 11.                    23497-5 Pa. $6.00

AMERICAN WILDLIFE AND PLANTS, A. C. Martin, et al. Describes food habits of more than 1000 species of mammals, birds, fish. Special treatment of important food plants. Over 300 illustrations. 500pp. 5⅜ x 8½.
20793-5 Pa. $4.95

THE PEOPLE CALLED SHAKERS, Edward D. Andrews. Lifetime of research, definitive study of Shakers: origins, beliefs, practices, dances, social organization, furniture and crafts, impact on 19th-century USA, present heritage. Indispensable to student of American history, collector. 33 illustrations. 351pp. 5⅜ x 8½.                    21081-2 Pa. $4.50

OLD NEW YORK IN EARLY PHOTOGRAPHS, Mary Black. New York City as it was in 1853-1901, through 196 wonderful photographs from N.-Y. Historical Society. Great Blizzard, Lincoln's funeral procession, great buildings. 228pp. 9 x 12.                    22907-6 Pa. $8.95

MR. LINCOLN'S CAMERA MAN: MATHEW BRADY, Roy Meredith. Over 300 Brady photos reproduced directly from original negatives, photos. Jackson, Webster, Grant, Lee, Carnegie, Barnum; Lincoln; Battle Smoke, Death of Rebel Sniper, Atlanta Just After Capture. Lively commentary. 368pp. 8⅜ x 11¼.                    23021-X Pa. $8.95

TRAVELS OF WILLIAM BARTRAM, William Bartram. From 1773-8, Bartram explored Northern Florida, Georgia, Carolinas, and reported on wild life, plants, Indians, early settlers. Basic account for period, entertaining reading. Edited by Mark Van Doren. 13 illustrations. 141pp. 5⅜ x 8½.                    20013-2 Pa. $5.00

THE GENTLEMAN AND CABINET MAKER'S DIRECTOR, Thomas Chippendale. Full reprint, 1762 style book, most influential of all time; chairs, tables, sofas, mirrors, cabinets, etc. 200 plates, plus 24 photographs of surviving pieces. 249pp. 9⅞ x 12¾.                    21601-2 Pa. $7.95

AMERICAN CARRIAGES, SLEIGHS, SULKIES AND CARTS, edited by Don H. Berkebile. 168 Victorian illustrations from catalogues, trade journals, fully captioned. Useful for artists. Author is Assoc. Curator, Div. of Transportation of Smithsonian Institution. 168pp. 8½ x 9½.
23328-6 Pa. $5.00

PRINCIPLES OF ORCHESTRATION, Nikolay Rimsky-Korsakov. Great classical orchestrator provides fundamentals of tonal resonance, progression of parts, voice and orchestra, tutti effects, much else in major document. 330pp. of musical excerpts. 489pp. 6½ x 9¼. 21266-1 Pa. $7.50

TRISTAN UND ISOLDE, Richard Wagner. Full orchestral score with complete instrumentation. Do not confuse with piano reduction. Commentary by Felix Mottl, great Wagnerian conductor and scholar. Study score. 655pp. 8⅛ x 11. 22915-7 Pa. $13.95

REQUIEM IN FULL SCORE, Giuseppe Verdi. Immensely popular with choral groups and music lovers. Republication of edition published by C. F. Peters, Leipzig, n. d. German frontmaker in English translation. Glossary. Text in Latin. Study score. 204pp. 9⅜ x 12¼.
23682-X Pa. $6.00

COMPLETE CHAMBER MUSIC FOR STRINGS, Felix Mendelssohn. All of Mendelssohn's chamber music: Octet, 2 Quintets, 6 Quartets, and Four Pieces for String Quartet. (Nothing with piano is included). Complete works edition (1874-7). Study score. 283 pp. 9⅜ x 12¼.
23679-X Pa. $7.50

POPULAR SONGS OF NINETEENTH-CENTURY AMERICA, edited by Richard Jackson. 64 most important songs: "Old Oaken Bucket," "Arkansas Traveler," "Yellow Rose of Texas," etc. Authentic original sheet music, full introduction and commentaries. 290pp. 9 x 12. 23270-0 Pa. $7.95

COLLECTED PIANO WORKS, Scott Joplin. Edited by Vera Brodsky Lawrence. Practically all of Joplin's piano works—rags, two-steps, marches, waltzes, etc., 51 works in all. Extensive introduction by Rudi Blesh. Total of 345pp. 9 x 12. 23106-2 Pa. $14.95

BASIC PRINCIPLES OF CLASSICAL BALLET, Agrippina Vaganova. Great Russian theoretician, teacher explains methods for teaching classical ballet; incorporates best from French, Italian, Russian schools. 118 illustrations. 175pp. 5⅜ x 8½. 22036-2 Pa. $2.50

CHINESE CHARACTERS, L. Wieger. Rich analysis of 2300 characters according to traditional systems into primitives. Historical-semantic analysis to phonetics (Classical Mandarin) and radicals. 820pp. 6⅛ x 9¼.
21321-8 Pa. $10.00

EGYPTIAN LANGUAGE: EASY LESSONS IN EGYPTIAN HIERO-GLYPHICS, E. A. Wallis Budge. Foremost Egyptologist offers Egyptian grammar, explanation of hieroglyphics, many reading texts, dictionary of symbols. 246pp. 5 x 7½. (Available in U.S. only)
21394-3 Clothbd. $7.50

AN ETYMOLOGICAL DICTIONARY OF MODERN ENGLISH, Ernest Weekley. Richest, fullest work, by foremost British lexicographer. Detailed word histories. Inexhaustible. Do not confuse this with *Concise Etymological Dictionary*, which is abridged. Total of 856pp. 6½ x 9¼.
21873-2, 21874-0 Pa., Two-vol. set $12.00

A MAYA GRAMMAR, Alfred M. Tozzer. Practical, useful English-language grammar by the Harvard anthropologist who was one of the three greatest American scholars in the area of Maya culture. Phonetics, grammatical processes, syntax, more. 301pp. 5⅜ x 8½. 23465-7 Pa. $4.00

THE JOURNAL OF HENRY D. THOREAU, edited by Bradford Torrey, F. H. Allen. Complete reprinting of 14 volumes, 1837-61, over two million words; the sourcebooks for Walden, etc. Definitive. All original sketches, plus 75 photographs. Introduction by Walter Harding. Total of 1804pp. 8½ x 12¼. 20312-3, 20313-1 Clothbd., Two-vol. set $70.00

CLASSIC GHOST STORIES, Charles Dickens and others. 18 wonderful stories you've wanted to reread: "The Monkey's Paw," "The House and the Brain," "The Upper Berth," "The Signalman," "Dracula's Guest," "The Tapestried Chamber," etc. Dickens, Scott, Mary Shelley, Stoker, etc. 330pp. 5⅜ x 8½. 20735-8 Pa. $4.50

SEVEN SCIENCE FICTION NOVELS, H. G. Wells. Full novels. First Men in the Moon, Island of Dr. Moreau, War of the Worlds, Food of the Gods, Invisible Man, Time Machine, In the Days of the Comet. A basic science-fiction library. 1015pp. 5⅜ x 8½. (Available in U.S. only) 20264-X Clothbd. $8.95

ARMADALE, Wilkie Collins. Third great mystery novel by the author of The Woman in White and The Moonstone. Ingeniously plotted narrative shows an exceptional command of character, incident and mood. Original magazine version with 40 illustrations. 597pp. 5⅜ x 8½. 23429-0 Pa. $6.00

MASTERS OF MYSTERY, H. Douglas Thomson. The first book in English (1931) devoted to history and aesthetics of detective story. Poe, Doyle, LeFanu, Dickens, many others, up to 1930. New introduction and notes by E. F. Bleiler. 288pp. 5⅜ x 8½. (Available in U.S. only) 23606-4 Pa. $4.00

FLATLAND, E. A. Abbott. Science-fiction classic explores life of 2-D being in 3-D world. Read also as introduction to thought about hyperspace. Introduction by Banesh Hoffmann. 16 illustrations. 103pp. 5⅜ x 8½. 20001-9 Pa. $2.00

THREE SUPERNATURAL NOVELS OF THE VICTORIAN PERIOD, edited, with an introduction, by E. F. Bleiler. Reprinted complete and unabridged, three great classics of the supernatural: The Haunted Hotel by Wilkie Collins, The Haunted House at Latchford by Mrs. J. H. Riddell, and The Lost Stradivarious by J. Meade Falkner. 325pp. 5⅜ x 8½. 22571-2 Pa. $4.00

AYESHA: THE RETURN OF "SHE," H. Rider Haggard. Virtuoso sequel featuring the great mythic creation, Ayesha, in an adventure that is fully as good as the first book, She. Original magazine version, with 47 original illustrations by Maurice Greiffenhagen. 189pp. 6½ x 9¼. 23649-8 Pa. $3.50

UNCLE SILAS, J. Sheridan LeFanu. Victorian Gothic mystery novel, considered by many best of period, even better than Collins or Dickens. Wonderful psychological terror. Introduction by Frederick Shroyer. 436pp. 5⅜ x 8½. 21715-9 Pa. $6.00

JURGEN, James Branch Cabell. The great erotic fantasy of the 1920's that delighted thousands, shocked thousands more. Full final text, Lane edition with 13 plates by Frank Pape. 346pp. 5⅜ x 8½.
23507-6 Pa. $4.50

THE CLAVERINGS, Anthony Trollope. Major novel, chronicling aspects of British Victorian society, personalities. Reprint of Cornhill serialization, 16 plates by M. Edwards; first reprint of full text. Introduction by Norman Donaldson. 412pp. 5⅜ x 8½. 23464-9 Pa. $5.00

KEPT IN THE DARK, Anthony Trollope. Unusual short novel about Victorian morality and abnormal psychology by the great English author. Probably the first American publication. Frontispiece by Sir John Millais. 92pp. 6½ x 9¼. 23609-9 Pa. $2.50

RALPH THE HEIR, Anthony Trollope. Forgotten tale of illegitimacy, inheritance. Master novel of Trollope's later years. Victorian country estates, clubs, Parliament, fox hunting, world of fully realized characters. Reprint of 1871 edition. 12 illustrations by F. A. Faser. 434pp. of text. 5⅜ x 8½. 23642-0 Pa. $5.00

YEKL and THE IMPORTED BRIDEGROOM AND OTHER STORIES OF THE NEW YORK GHETTO, Abraham Cahan. Film *Hester Street* based on *Yekl* (1896). Novel, other stories among first about Jewish immigrants of N.Y.'s East Side. Highly praised by W. D. Howells—Cahan "a new star of realism." New introduction by Bernard G. Richards. 240pp. 5⅜ x 8½. 22427-9 Pa. $3.50

THE HIGH PLACE, James Branch Cabell. Great fantasy writer's enchanting comedy of disenchantment set in 18th-century France. Considered by some critics to be even better than his famous *Jurgen*. 10 illustrations and numerous vignettes by noted fantasy artist Frank C. Pape. 320pp. 5⅜ x 8½. 23670-6 Pa. $4.00

ALICE'S ADVENTURES UNDER GROUND, Lewis Carroll. Facsimile of ms. Carroll gave Alice Liddell in 1864. Different in many ways from final Alice. Handlettered, illustrated by Carroll. Introduction by Martin Gardner. 128pp. 5⅜ x 8½. 21482-6 Pa. $2.50

FAVORITE ANDREW LANG FAIRY TALE BOOKS IN MANY COLORS, Andrew Lang. The four Lang favorites in a boxed set—the complete *Red, Green, Yellow* and *Blue* Fairy Books. 164 stories; 439 illustrations by Lancelot Speed, Henry Ford and G. P. Jacomb Hood. Total of about 1500pp. 5⅜ x 8½. 23407-X Boxed set, Pa. $15.95

HOUSEHOLD STORIES BY THE BROTHERS GRIMM. All the great Grimm stories: "Rumpelstiltskin," "Snow White," "Hansel and Gretel," etc., with 114 illustrations by Walter Crane. 269pp. 5⅜ x 8½.
21080-4 Pa. $3.50

SLEEPING BEAUTY, illustrated by Arthur Rackham. Perhaps the fullest, most delightful version ever, told by C. S. Evans. Rackham's best work. 49 illustrations. 110pp. 7⅞ x 10¾.
22756-1 Pa. $2.50

AMERICAN FAIRY TALES, L. Frank Baum. Young cowboy lassoes Father Time; dummy in Mr. Floman's department store window comes to life; and 10 other fairy tales. 41 illustrations by N. P. Hall, Harry Kennedy, Ike Morgan, and Ralph Gardner. 209pp. 5⅜ x 8½.
23643-9 Pa. $3.00

THE WONDERFUL WIZARD OF OZ, L. Frank Baum. Facsimile in full color of America's finest children's classic. Introduction by Martin Gardner. 143 illustrations by W. W. Denslow. 267pp. 5⅜ x 8½.
20691-2 Pa. $3.50

THE TALE OF PETER RABBIT, Beatrix Potter. The inimitable Peter's terrifying adventure in Mr. McGregor's garden, with all 27 wonderful, full-color Potter illustrations. 55pp. 4¼ x 5½. (Available in U.S. only)
22827-4 Pa. $1.25

THE STORY OF KING ARTHUR AND HIS KNIGHTS, Howard Pyle. Finest children's version of life of King Arthur. 48 illustrations by Pyle. 131pp. 6⅛ x 9¼.
21445-1 Pa. $4.95

CARUSO'S CARICATURES, Enrico Caruso. Great tenor's remarkable caricatures of self, fellow musicians, composers, others. Toscanini, Puccini, Farrar, etc. Impish, cutting, insightful. 473 illustrations. Preface by M. Sisca. 217pp. 8⅜ x 11¼.
23528-9 Pa. $6.95

PERSONAL NARRATIVE OF A PILGRIMAGE TO ALMADINAH AND MECCAH, Richard Burton. Great travel classic by remarkably colorful personality. Burton, disguised as a Moroccan, visited sacred shrines of Islam, narrowly escaping death. Wonderful observations of Islamic life, customs, personalities. 47 illustrations. Total of 959pp. 5⅜ x 8½.
21217-3, 21218-1 Pa., Two-vol. set $12.00

INCIDENTS OF TRAVEL IN YUCATAN, John L. Stephens. Classic (1843) exploration of jungles of Yucatan, looking for evidences of Maya civilization. Travel adventures, Mexican and Indian culture, etc. Total of 669pp. 5⅜ x 8½.
20926-1, 20927-X Pa., Two-vol. set $7.90

AMERICAN LITERARY AUTOGRAPHS FROM WASHINGTON IRVING TO HENRY JAMES, Herbert Cahoon, et al. Letters, poems, manuscripts of Hawthorne, Thoreau, Twain, Alcott, Whitman, 67 other prominent American authors. Reproductions, full transcripts and commentary. Plus checklist of all American Literary Autographs in The Pierpont Morgan Library. Printed on exceptionally high-quality paper. 136 illustrations. 212pp. 9⅛ x 12¼.
23548-3 Pa. $12.50

AN AUTOBIOGRAPHY, Margaret Sanger. Exciting personal account of hard-fought battle for woman's right to birth control, against prejudice, church, law. Foremost feminist document. 504pp. 5⅜ x 8½.
20470-7 Pa. $5.50

MY BONDAGE AND MY FREEDOM, Frederick Douglass. Born as a slave, Douglass became outspoken force in antislavery movement. The best of Douglass's autobiographies. Graphic description of slave life. Introduction by P. Foner. 464pp. 5⅜ x 8½.
22457-0 Pa. $5.50

LIVING MY LIFE, Emma Goldman. Candid, no holds barred account by foremost American anarchist: her own life, anarchist movement, famous contemporaries, ideas and their impact. Struggles and confrontations in America, plus deportation to U.S.S.R. Shocking inside account of persecution of anarchists under Lenin. 13 plates. Total of 944pp. 5⅜ x 8½.
22543-7, 22544-5 Pa., Two-vol. set $12.00

LETTERS AND NOTES ON THE MANNERS, CUSTOMS AND CONDITIONS OF THE NORTH AMERICAN INDIANS, George Catlin. Classic account of life among Plains Indians: ceremonies, hunt, warfare, etc. Dover edition reproduces for first time all original paintings. 312 plates. 572pp. of text. 6⅛ x 9¼.
22118-0, 22119-9 Pa.. Two-vol. set $12.00

THE MAYA AND THEIR NEIGHBORS, edited by Clarence L. Hay, others. Synoptic view of Maya civilization in broadest sense, together with Northern, Southern neighbors. Integrates much background, valuable detail not elsewhere. Prepared by greatest scholars: Kroeber, Morley, Thompson, Spinden, Vaillant, many others. Sometimes called Tozzer Memorial Volume. 60 illustrations, linguistic map. 634pp. 5⅜ x 8½.
23510-6 Pa. $10.00

HANDBOOK OF THE INDIANS OF CALIFORNIA, A. L. Kroeber. Foremost American anthropologist offers complete ethnographic study of each group. Monumental classic. 459 illustrations, maps. 995pp. 5⅜ x 8½.
23368-5 Pa. $13.00

SHAKTI AND SHAKTA, Arthur Avalon. First book to give clear, cohesive analysis of Shakta doctrine, Shakta ritual and Kundalini Shakti (yoga). Important work by one of world's foremost students of Shaktic and Tantric thought. 732pp. 5⅜ x 8½. (Available in U.S. only)
23645-5 Pa. $7.95

AN INTRODUCTION TO THE STUDY OF THE MAYA HIEROGLYPHS, Syvanus Griswold Morley. Classic study by one of the truly great figures in hieroglyph research. Still the best introduction for the student for reading Maya hieroglyphs. New introduction by J. Eric S. Thompson. 117 illustrations. 284pp. 5⅜ x 8½.
23108-9 Pa. $4.00

A STUDY OF MAYA ART, Herbert J. Spinden. Landmark classic interprets Maya symbolism, estimates styles, covers ceramics, architecture, murals, stone carvings as artforms. Still a basic book in area. New introduction by J. Eric Thompson. Over 750 illustrations. 341pp. 8⅜ x 11¼.
21235-1 Pa. $6.95

AMERICAN ANTIQUE FURNITURE, Edgar G. Miller, Jr. The basic coverage of all American furniture before 1840: chapters per item chronologically cover all types of furniture, with more than 2100 photos. Total of 1106pp. 7⅞ x 10¾.　　　21599-7, 21600-4 Pa., Two-vol. set $17.90

ILLUSTRATED GUIDE TO SHAKER FURNITURE, Robert Meader. Director, Shaker Museum, Old Chatham, presents up-to-date coverage of all furniture and appurtenances, with much on local styles not available elsewhere. 235 photos. 146pp. 9 x 12.　　　22819-3 Pa. $6.00

ORIENTAL RUGS, ANTIQUE AND MODERN, Walter A. Hawley. Persia, Turkey, Caucasus, Central Asia, China, other traditions. Best general survey of all aspects: styles and periods, manufacture, uses, symbols and their interpretation, and identification. 96 illustrations, 11 in color. 320pp. 6⅛ x 9¼.　　　22366-3 Pa. $6.95

CHINESE POTTERY AND PORCELAIN, R. L. Hobson. Detailed descriptions and analyses by former Keeper of the Department of Oriental Antiquities and Ethnography at the British Museum. Covers hundreds of pieces from primitive times to 1915. Still the standard text for most periods. 136 plates, 40 in full color. Total of 750pp. 5⅝ x 8½.
23253-0 Pa. $10.00

THE WARES OF THE MING DYNASTY, R. L. Hobson. Foremost scholar examines and illustrates many varieties of Ming (1368-1644). Famous blue and white, polychrome, lesser-known styles and shapes. 117 illustrations, 9 full color, of outstanding pieces. Total of 263pp. 6⅛ x 9¼. (Available in U.S. only)　　　23652-8 Pa. $6.00